THE BOOK OF
ENOCH

MODERN STANDARD VERSION

MSV

Translated from the Ethiopic version and edited from twenty-three manuscripts together with the fragmentary Greek and Latin versions by R. H. Charles, D.LITT., D.D.

Additional translation by: Richard Laurence, George H. Schodde, and August Dillmann

KIP FARRAR

edited by:
JUNE HEINZE

www.enochmsv.com

CONTENTS

THE BOOK OF ENOCH THE PROPHET

REFERENCE

WHY READ THE BOOK OF ENOCH

Many scholars once thought the Book of Enoch was written after the New Testament simply because the parallels were too great. It had to be written after. But the Dead Sea Scrolls and other writings proved the Book of Enoch came first.

This means nearly all of the New Testament writers were influenced by Enoch in their writing of scripture because Enoch is heavily reflected in their work. Even Jesus Christ alludes to images, themes, and ideas from this book. Enoch was part of Jewish tradition at the time and is just one of many outside works alluded to in the Holy Bible.

(Not to be confused with the hoax writings in the Slavonic Enoch called The Secrets of Enoch/2 Enoch or the Hebrew Enoch called The Revelation of Metatron/3 Enoch. These post-New Testament works have nothing to do with the Book of Enoch and are proven fabrications.)

The Holy Bible can be fully read and understood on its own, but the Book of Enoch brings greater clarity and context to confusing passages and ideas. For example, Revelation is often considered one of the most perplexing books of the Bible, and much of Revelation is an adapted retelling of the Book of Enoch.

Most importantly, the Book of Enoch does not bring new revelation to the Holy Bible. It does not alter or recontextualize scripture. Every idea and theme from Enoch is already present in the Bible. This work can be studied to great benefit without fear of tainted doctrine.

PREFACE

The MSV Approach

The Modern Standard Version allows you to experience the Book of Enoch in a form updated for the modern reader. Many archaic words in the adapted translations are replaced in the MSV while preserving the intended meaning. If there was doubt about the consequences of updating a word, the change was marked with a footnote.

The authoritative Ethiopic translation of R. H. Charles is combined in the MSV with the translations of Richard Laurence, George H. Schodde, and August Dillmann to make the text easier to understand, such as with proper angel names. The Holy Bible often takes names such as Yeshua and transliterates them into something easier to say (in this case, Yeshua became Jesus). As such, the MSV uses the work of Richard Laurence and others to create an easier reading experience. Some of these changes are marked with footnotes.

The extensive notes from the translators enhanced the cross-references in the MSV to the Holy Bible. All four translations and their notes were diligently compared when updating the text.

FEATURES OF THIS EDITION

Section Headings

Throughout the MSV, section headings are included with the text. These headings are not part of the Enoch manuscripts, but are included for ease of identifying sections and themes.

Translation Footnotes

The translation of R. H. Charles is replaced with modern terminology and sentence structure, mostly for clarity and proper names. These are sometimes indicated by footnotes, which are detailed at the bottom of each page. A footnote is marked by a superscript [1] number that follows the word or phrase it denotes.

Cross-Reference Footnotes

Many passages in the Holy Bible can be cross-referenced with the Book of Enoch. These cross-references are not usually intended to show a direct relationship between the verses, but to demonstrate the consistency of ideas and themes between the Holy Bible and the Book of Enoch. These are indicated by footnotes.

Parallel Passages

In the back of the book is a section on parallel passages to the New Testament of the Holy Bible. These have been included from the works of both R. H. Charles and Richard Laurence.

ON BOOKS, CHAPTERS, AND VERSES

The Book of Enoch is pieced together from fragments written in different languages, and most (or all) of those fragments are not in the text's original language. This means the translators struggled to find verses and words moved out of order or duplicated across the centuries. So the verse numbers you see will occasionally be out of order.

Other ancient texts have been discovered that falsely claim a connection to Enoch. One is the Slavonic Enoch, also called The Secrets of Enoch. Another work is the Hebrew Enoch, also called The Revelation of Metatron. Both of these fictional works were created after the birth of Christianity and had no connection to the ancient person of Enoch or to the Book of Enoch. Scholars labeled these works 2 Enoch and 3 Enoch for academic distinction, but this is confusing and creates the false impression that all three works are connected. We should now erase these ties.

Within the true Book of Enoch are five traditional books, each with a distinctive name (such as the book of The Watchers). The Modern Standard Version seeks to streamline the presentation of the Book of Enoch in a form familiar and comfortable to readers of the Holy Bible. The traditional five books are here divided into eight parts, labeled 1 Enoch through 8 Enoch, while keeping the traditional titles as subtitles. This update should make the varying sections more palatable and easier to understand.

ON STYLE

After years of translating the Book of Enoch, R. H. Charles was delighted to discover that the book was written in prose. It helped him restore missing elements of the text and aided in his translation of unusual sentence structure.

In the Holy Bible, the books of Job and Psalms are written this way. A similar presentation style is repeated here to recapture the lyrical feel of the original writing.

Words in *italics* are not in the original text, but their meaning is implied. These are included for clarity and an easier reading experience.

The Book of Enoch the Prophet

.

Modern Standard Version

1 ENOCH

The Watchers

1 THE WORDS of the blessing of Enoch, that he used to bless the chosen and righteous,[1] who will be living in the day of tribulation, when all the wicked and godless are removed.

A Blessing

2 He took up his declaration saying, "Enoch, a righteous man whose eyes were opened by God, saw the vision of the Holy One in the heavens. The angels showed me, and I heard everything from them. I understood what they showed me,[2] but *it was* not for this generation, but for a distant one that is still to come."

3 I spoke about the chosen,
    and took up my declaration about them:
"The Holy Great One will leave His dwelling,
4   and the eternal God will walk on the earth,
even on Mount Sinai;
    and appear with His host,[3]
and appear in the strength of His might
    from the heaven of heavens.
5 Fear will strike everyone;
    the watchers[4] will quake;

---

1 Compare Deu 33:1 - *the blessing of Moses*
2 Compare Rev 1:1 - *He made it known by sending his angel to his servant John*
3 Or *from his camp*
4 Compare Dan 4:13, 17, 23 ESV - *a watcher, a holy one, came down from heaven.*

> great fear and trembling will seize them
>> unto the ends of the earth.

6   The high mountains will shake,
>> the high hills will be made low,
>> and will melt like wax before the flame.[1]

7   The earth will be wholly torn apart.
>> All that is on the earth will perish,
>> and there will be judgment over all.

8   But with the righteous, He will make peace.
>> *He* will protect the chosen,
>> and mercy will be on them.
> They will all belong to God,
>> they will prosper,
>> and they will all be blessed.
> He will help them all,
>> light will appear to them,
>> and He will make peace with them."[2]

9   "Behold, the Lord comes with ten thousands of His holy
>> ones,
> to execute judgment on all
> and to convict all the ungodly
>> of all their deeds of ungodliness
> that they committed in such an ungodly way,
>> and of all the harsh things that ungodly sinners have
>> spoken against Him."[3]

---

1 Compare Psa 97:3-5 - *The earth sees and trembles... The mountains melt like wax before the Lord*

2 Compare Psa 97:11 - *Light is sown for the righteous, and joy*

3 Jude 1:14-15 ESV (Direct quote, with attribution to Enoch himself)

Observe Heaven and Earth

2 "WATCH EVERYTHING that takes place in the heavens,
   how they do not change their orbits,
      and the lights that are in the heavens;
   how they all rise and set in order, each in its season,
      and do not violate their appointed order.*[1]*

2   Watch the earth, and pay attention to the things that
               take place on it from first to last,
         how reliable they are,
      how none of the things on earth change,
               but all the works of God appear to you.

3   Watch the summer and the winter,
         how the whole earth is filled with water,
         and clouds and dew and mist lie upon it."

Observe the Trees

3 "WATCH AND see how in the winter all the trees seem as
   though they had withered and shed all their leaves,
      except fourteen trees, that do not lose their foliage,
         but keep the old foliage for two to three years
         until the new comes."

Observe Summer

4 "AGAIN, SEE the days of summer,
   how the sun is above the earth's horizon.
      You seek shade and shelter because of the heat of the sun,
         and the earth also burns with growing heat,
      so you cannot tread on the earth,
         or on a rock because of its heat."

---

1 Compare Jer 31:35-36 - *fixed order*

The Elect Will Inherit the Earth

5 "SEE HOW the trees cover themselves with green leaves and
    bear fruit:
    so pay attention carefully and know about all of His works,
        and recognize that Him who lives forever[1] made them that way.

2   All His works go on this way.
        from year to year forever,
    and all the tasks that they accomplish for Him—and their
            tasks do not change,
        but according as God has ordained, so is it done.

3   See how the sea and the rivers also perform
        and do not change their tasks from his commandments.

4   But you—you have not been faithful,
        nor followed the commandments of the Lord,
    but you have turned away and spoken proud and hard
        words with your impure mouths against His greatness.
    Oh you hard-hearted, you will find no peace."

5   "Therefore you will curse your days,
        the years of your life will perish,
        and the years of your destruction will be multiplied in
            eternal curses.
        You will find no mercy.

6   In those days, you will make your names an eternal
            curse to all the righteous,
    and by you all who curse will curse,
        and all the sinners and godless will curse by you,
        and for you wicked there will be a curse.[2]
    All the *chosen* will rejoice,
        and there will be forgiveness of sins,

---

1 Compare Rev 10:6 - *him who lives forever and ever*
2 This line was formerly the last line of verse 7 - *And for you wicked*

and every mercy and peace and reprieve;
>   there will be salvation to them, a good light.
There will be no salvation for all you sinners,
>   but a curse will stay on you all.
7   But for the chosen there will be light, joy, and peace,
>   and they will inherit the earth." [1]

8   "Then the chosen will receive wisdom,
>   and they will all live and never again sin, [2]
neither through ungodliness nor through pride;
>   but they who are wise will be humble.
9   They will not disobey again,
>   nor will they sin all the days of their lives,
nor will they die of *my righteous* anger or wrath,
>   but they will complete the full days of their lives.
Their lives will be increased in peace,
>   and the years of their joy will be multiplied
in eternal gladness and peace
>   all the days of their lives."

Angels Descend

6 IT CAME to pass when the children of men had multiplied,
that in those days were born unto them beautiful and
>   attractive daughters.
2   The angels, the children of the heavens,
>   saw and lusted after them, saying to one another,
"Come, let us choose wives from among the daughters
>   of men, and father children." [3]
3   Samyaza, who was their leader, said to them,

---

1 Compare Mat 5:5 - *Blessed are the meek, for they shall inherit the earth*
2 Compare Zeph 3:11-13 ASV - *The remnant of Israel will do no wrong*
3 Compare Gen 6:1-4; Jude 1:6; 1Co 11:10 - *The Nephilim*

> "I fear you won't actually agree to this act,
> and I alone must pay the penalty of a great sin."

4   They all answered him, saying,
> "Let us all swear an oath
> and all bind ourselves by mutual curses
> not to abandon this plan but to do this thing."

5   Then they all swore together and bound themselves by
> mutual curses upon it.[1]

6   They were two hundred total who descended in the days of
> Jared[2] on the summit of Mount Hermon,[3]
> and they called it Mount Hermon, because they had sworn and
> bound themselves by mutual curses upon it.[4]

7   These are the names of their leaders:[5] Samyaza, their leader, Urakaba, Rameel, Akibeel, Tamiel, Ramuel, Danel, Ziquel, Baraqel, Azazel, Armaros, Matarel, Ananel, Setawel, Shamshiel, Sahriel, Ertael, Turel, Tumael, and Yomyael.

8   These are their commanders of tens.

Giants on the Earth

7 THEY AND all the others with them took for themselves wives, each choosing for himself one.
> They went to *their wives* and defiled themselves with them.
> They taught them charms, enchantments,[6] and the
> cutting of roots
> and made them acquainted with plants.

---

1 Compare Eph 6:12 KJV - *spiritual wickedness in high places*
2 *Jared*; Gen 5:18-20; The name Jared means *Shall come down*
3 Also known as the *Mountain of Bashan*. See Psa 68:15, 16
4 Compare Mar 9:2; Luk 9:28-29 - *Jesus transfigured on Mt. Hermon*
5 Angel names required extensive reconstruction. The Holy Bible lists many names of satanic powers such as Lucifer, Apollyon, Baal, and many others.
6 Compare Isa 47:7-10

2   *The women* became pregnant and gave birth to great
                giants,[1]
         giving birth to three kinds.
     First came Titans, whose height was three hundred cubits;[2]
         the Titans fathered the Nephilim,
     and to the Nephilim were born the Eliud,
         and they grew according to their greatness.
3   *The giants* consumed everything man had.
     When men could no longer sustain them,
4   the giants turned against them,
         devouring mankind.[3]
5   *The giants* sinned against birds, beasts, reptiles, and fish,
         devoured each other's flesh,
         and drank their blood.
6   Then the earth laid accusation against the lawless ones.

False Teachers

8 AZAZEL[4] TAUGHT men to make swords,[5] knives, shields,
                and breastplates.[6]
     He made known to them the metals of the earth and the
                art of working them,
         and bracelets, ornaments, and the use of antimony,
     and the beautifying of the eyelids, and all kinds of costly stones,
                and all coloring dyes.

---

1 Compare Num 13:33; 1Sa 17:4, 7
2 Laurence: *about 450ft.*
3 Compare Num 13:32 - *a land that devours its inhabitants, and all the people that we saw in it are of great height*
4 Spelling of *Azazel* from the Holy Bible. See Lev 16:8, 10, 26 ESV
5 Compare Isa 54:16 - *It is I* (the Lord) *who have created the blacksmith who fans coals in the fire, and produces a weapon for his purpose.* Note that these teachings are taken from heaven (Enoch 16:3) but are used for evil. See Num 22:23: the angel of the LORD holds a sword; Rev 9:17: Heavenly troops with breastplates.
6 These teachings are also ascribed to a *satan* named *Gadrel* in Enoch 69:6

2   Godlessness became widespread;
        they committed fornication;
    they were led astray,
        and became corrupt in all their ways.

3   Samyaza taught drug magic and root-cuttings,[1]
        and Armaros, the application of sorcery.[2]
    Baraqel *taught* astrology, Akibeel the constellations,
        Ziquel the knowledge of the clouds, Rameel[3] the signs
            of the earth,
    Shamshiel the signs of the sun, and Sahriel the course of
            the moon.
    And as men perished, they cried *out,*[4]
        and their cry went up to heaven . . .[5]

Angels Seek Justice

9 THEN MICHAEL, Sariel, Raphael, and Gabriel looked down from heaven and saw considerable bloodshed on the earth, and all lawlessness being done on the earth.

2   They said to one another:
        "The earth, deprived of its inhabitants,
    cries up[6] to the gates of heaven because of the voice of
            their outcry.[7]
3   Now to you, the holy ones of heaven,
        the souls of men make their plea,

---

1 Or *enchantments and pharmakeía*
2 Compare Exo 7:11, 12 - *sorcerers... magicians... secret arts*
3 Or *Araqiêl*
4 Compare 2Pe 2:1-4 - *angels when they sinned*
5 Missing passage
6 Compare Isa 26:21 - *the earth will disclose the blood shed on it*
7 Compare Lev 18:27, 28 - *lest the land vomit you out when you make it unclean*

saying, 'Bring our cause before the Most High.' " [1]

4   And they said to the Lord of the ages,
        "Lord of lords, God of gods, King of kings,[2] and God of
            the ages,
    the throne of Your glory *stands* unto all the generations of the ages,
    and Your name is holy, glorious, and blessed unto all the ages!"

5   "You have made all things,
        and You have power over all things.
    All things are naked and open in Your sight.
    You see all things, and nothing can hide itself from You." [3]

6   "You see what Azazel has done,
        who has taught all unrighteousness on earth
    and revealed the eternal secrets that were *kept* in heaven,
        that men were striving to learn.
7   And *You see what* Samyaza *has done*, to whom You have
            given authority to rule over his associates:
8   they have gone to the daughters of men on the earth;
    they have slept with the women and defiled themselves,
        and revealed to them all kinds of sins.
9   The women have given birth to giants,[4]
        so the whole earth has been filled with blood and
            unrighteousness.
10   Now look, the souls of the dead are crying *out*

---

1 Compare Heb 1:14 - *Are they not all ministering spirits sent out to serve for the sake of those who are to inherit salvation?*; While humanity does not pray to angels in the Holy Bible, an angel does present the prayers of believers to God in Rev 8:3-4 - *the prayers of the saints, rose before God from the hand of the angel*
2 Compare Rev 17:14; 19:16 - *King of kings and Lord of lords*
3 Compare Heb 4:13 - *all are naked and exposed to the eyes of him*
4 Compare 2Sa 21:15-22; Deu 3:11; Amo 2:9

and seeking justice to the gates of heaven.[1]
Their grievances have ascended,
and cannot stop because of the lawless deeds
that are done on the earth.[2]

11   You know all things before they come to pass.
You see these things, and You endure them,
and You say nothing to us about how to respond to the
people." [3]

The Flood Foretold

10 THEN THE Most High proclaimed,
the Holy and Great One spoke,
and sent Sariel[4] to the son of Lamech, saying,

2   "Go to Noah, and tell him in My name,[5]
'Hide yourself!'[6]
Reveal to him the end that is approaching,
that the whole earth will be destroyed.
A flood is about to come on the whole earth,[7]
and will destroy all that is on it.
3   Now instruct him so he may escape
and his seed may be preserved
for all the generations of the world."

4   Again the Lord said to Raphael,

---

1 Compare Gen 4:10; Rev 6:10 - *how long before you will judge and avenge our blood*
2 Compare Rev 6:9, 10
3 Compare 2Pe 2:11
4 Or *Arsayalalyur*
5 This is an occurrence separate from God's word to Noah in Gen 6:13-21; For example, God gave similar words to Abraham on different occasions.
6 Compare Isa 26:20 - *hide yourselves... until the fury has passed by*
7 Compare Gen 7:17-24 - *The flood continued forty days... all flesh died*

"Bind Azazel hand and foot,
and cast him into the darkness.
Make an opening in the desert of Dudael,
and cast him in.

5 Place rough and jagged rocks on him,
and cover him with darkness;
let him stay there forever,
and cover his face that he may not see light.

6 On the day of the great judgment, he will be cast
into the fire.
Heal the earth that the angels have corrupted,
and announce the cleansing of the earth,
that I may heal the plague;

7 that all the children of men may not perish
through the secret things the watchers have
uncovered and taught to their sons.[1]

8 The whole earth has been corrupted
through the works taught by Azazel:
accuse him of every sin."[2]

9 To Gabriel, the Lord said:
"Move against the bastards, the cross-breeds,
and against the children of unnatural union.
Destroy the children of fornication and the children
of the watchers from among men
and drive them out.
Turn them against each other so they destroy one
another in battle,
for they will not have a long life.

---

1 Compare 2Pe 2:1-6; Paul correlates the angels who sinned with false teachers and the sexual sins of Sodom and Gomorrah.
2 Compare Lev 16:8-10 ESV - *the goat on which the lot fell for Azazel shall be presented alive before the LORD to make atonement over it*

10   Though they will plead to you,

        their fathers will secure nothing for them.

    Although *the giants* expect an everlasting life,

        they won't have even five hundred years."[1]

11   And the Lord said to Michael,

    "Go, bind Samyaza and his associates who have united

        themselves with women,

    and have defiled themselves with them in all their

        uncleanness.

12   When their sons have killed one another,

        and they have seen the destruction of their beloved ones,

    bind them fast for seventy generations[2] in the valleys of

        the earth,

    until the day of their judgment and of their fulfillment,

    until the judgment that is forever and ever

        is consummated." [3]

13   "In those days, they will be taken to the abyss of fire,

        to *their* torment, and to the prison where they will be

        confined forever.[4]

14   Whoever is condemned and destroyed from then on

        will be bound together with them

        to the end of all generations.

15   Destroy all the chimera[5] spirits

        and the children of the watchers,

---

1 Compare Gen 5; Lifespans at this time often reached 900 years.

2 Compare Luke 3:23-37; There are 70 generations from Enoch to Jesus.

3 Compare 1Pe 3:18-20 - *Christ... being put to death in the flesh but made alive in the spirit, in which he went and proclaimed to the spirits in prison, because they formerly did not obey, when God's patience waited in the days of Noah, while the ark was being prepared*

4 Compare Rev 20:10 - *they will be tormented day and night forever and ever*

5 Or *cross-breed*; lit. *counterfeit*

because they have wronged mankind.

16 Destroy all wrong from the face of the earth,
  let every evil work come to an end,
  and let the plant of righteousness[1] and truth appear.
It will prove a blessing.
The works of righteousness and truth
  will be planted in truth and joy forever."

17 "Then all the righteous will escape,
  will live until they father thousands of children,
and all the days of their youth and their old age
  they will complete in peace.
18 The whole earth will be tilled in righteousness,
  will be planted with trees, and be full of blessing.
19 All desirable trees will be planted on it,
  and they will plant vines on it;
the vine they plant on it will make wine in abundance,
  and as for all the seed that is sown on it,
each measure *of it* will make a thousand,
  and each measure of olives will make ten presses of oil."

20 "Cleanse the earth from all oppression,
  from all unrighteousness,
  from all sin, and from all godlessness.
All the uncleanness that is done on the earth—
  destroy from off the earth.[2]
21 All the children of men will become righteous;[3]
  all nations will offer adoration, will praise Me,

---

1 *plant of righteousness*: Israel; See Enoch 62:8, 84:6, 93:2,5,10
2 Referring to the great flood
3 Peter in 1Pe 3:20-21 compares the flood of Noah to baptism. See Heb 11:7 -
Noah... became an heir of the righteousness that comes by faith

and all will worship Me.[1]

22   The earth will be cleansed from all defilement,
        all sin, all punishment, and from all torment,[2]
     and I will never again send *a world-wide flood* on it
        from generation to generation and forever."[3]

Blessings From Heaven

1 1   "IN THOSE days, I will open the store chambers of blessing
     that are in heaven,
        to send them down on the earth over the work and labor of the
            children of men.[4]

2   Truth and peace will be associated together
        throughout all the days of the world
     and throughout all the generations of men."

Enoch the Scribe

1 2   BEFORE THESE things, Enoch was hidden. None of the
     children of men knew where he was hidden, or where he
dwelled, or what had become of him. 2 His activities involved the
watchers,[5] and his days were spent with the holy ones.

3   I, Enoch was blessing the Lord of majesty, and the King of the

---

1 Compare Isa 2:2-4, Zec 13:1, 2; 14:6
2 Compare Gen 3:17 - *cursed is the ground because of you*; God removes this
curse in Gen 8:21 - *the LORD said in his heart, "I will never again curse the ground
because of man"*; Gen 5:29 - *and called his name Noah, saying, "Out of the ground
that the LORD has cursed, this one shall bring us relief from our work and from the
painful toil of our hands."*
3 Compare Gen 8:21: - *Neither will I ever again strike down every living creature*
4 Compare Mal 3:10 - *windows of heaven... blessing*
5 Compare Dan 4:13, 17, 23 ESV - *a watcher*

ages, and look! the *holy* watchers[1] called me—Enoch the scribe—
saying to me:

4   "Enoch, you scribe of righteousness,
          go, declare to the *fallen* watchers of the heavens
       who have left the high heaven, the holy eternal place,
          have defiled themselves with women,
       have done as the children of *the* earth do,
          and have taken to themselves wives:
       'You have worked great destruction on the earth.
5   You will have no peace or forgiveness of sin.'
       To the extent they delight themselves in their children,
6   so they will see the murder of their beloved ones.
       They will lament over the destruction of their children,
          and will make pleas until eternity,
       'But you will not have mercy or peace.'"

Fate of the Watchers

13 AND ENOCH, departing, said,
       "Azazel, you will have no peace.
       A severe sentence has gone out against you
          to put you in chains.
2   You will not have leniency nor request granted to you,
          because of the unrighteousness that you have taught,
       and because of all the works of godlessness, unrighteousness,
          and sin that you have revealed to men."
3   Then I went and spoke to them all together,
          and they were all afraid;
          fear and trembling seized them.
4   They begged me to draw up a petition for them so they might
                find forgiveness,

---

1 *Watchers* can apply to either holy angels or fallen angels. In this case, holy
ones. See Dan 4:13, 17, 23 ESV - *a watcher, a holy one, came down from heaven.*

and to read their petition in the presence of the Lord of Heaven.

5   Because they could no longer lift up their voices or their eyes to
            heaven[1]
      on account of the shame and condemnation of their sins.

6   Then I wrote out their petition and their prayers about their
            individual deeds and beloved ones,
      and about their requests for forgiveness and longevity.

7   I went off and sat down at the waters of Dan,
            in the land of Dan to the southwest of Hermon,
      and I read *aloud* their petition until I fell asleep.

8   Behold, a dream came to me, and visions fell down on me.
      I saw visions of rebuke.
      A voice came commanding *me* to recount *this vision*
            to the sons of heaven, and reprimand them.

9   When I awoke, I came to them.
      They were all sitting gathered together, weeping in Oubelseyael,
            which is between Lebanon and Seneser.
            And their faces *were* covered.

10   I described, in their presence, all the visions that I saw while asleep.
      I spoke the words of righteousness
            and the reprimand of the heavenly watchers.

The Book of the Words of Righteousness

14 THE BOOK of the words of righteousness, and of the
      reprimand of the eternal watchers according to the command
of the Holy Great One in that vision.

2   I saw in my sleep what I will now say with a tongue of flesh

---

1 Compare Joh 9:31 - *We know that God does not listen to sinners, but if anyone
is a worshiper of God and does his will, God listens to him;* Jer 14:12 - *Though they
fast, I will not hear their cry*

and with the breath of my mouth,
that the Great One has given to men to speak with
and *thus* understand with the heart.

3   As He has created and given to man
the power of understanding the word of wisdom,
so has He created me also
and given me the power of reprimanding the watchers,
the children of heaven. *1*

4   I wrote out your petition, and in my vision it appeared like this:
your petition will not be granted to you
throughout all the days of eternity. *2*
Indeed, it will not be granted;
judgment has finally been passed on you.

5   From now on, you will not ascend into heaven until all eternity.
The order has been decreed beneath the earth
to chain you for all the days of the world.

6   Before all this, you will see the destruction of your beloved sons.
You will have no pleasure in them;
they will fall before you by the sword.

7   Your petition on their behalf will not be granted,
nor the one for yourselves,
even though you weep and pray over all the words
contained in the writing that I have written.

8   The vision was shown to me like this:
Behold, in the vision, clouds called to me; *3*
a mist summoned me.

---

1 Compare 1Co 6:3 - *Do you not know that we are to judge angels?*
2 Compare Jer 11:14 - *do not pray for this people, or lift up a cry or prayer on their behalf, for I will not listen when they call to me in the time of their trouble.*
3 Compare Exo 24:16 - *called to Moses out of the midst of the cloud*

Shooting stars and flashes of lighting
  propelled and accelerated me.
The winds in the vision caused me to fly,
  lifted me upward, and carried me into heaven.[1]

9   I kept going until I drew close to a wall
  that was built of crystals and surrounded by tongues of fire,
  and it frightened me.

10   I went into the tongues of fire and drew close to a large house
  that was built of crystals.
The walls of the house were like a crystal mosaic,
  and it had crystal groundwork.

11   Its ceiling was like the paths of shooting stars and flashes of
          lightning;
  among them were fiery cherubim,
  and the expanse above *the cherubim* was as *clear as* water.[2]

12   A flaming fire surrounded the walls,
  and its portals blazed with fire.

13   I entered into that house;
  it was hot as fire and cold as ice;
  there were no delights of life in that place.
Fear covered me; trembling took hold on me.

14   As I quaked and trembled, I fell on my face.

15   I saw a vision, and look! there was a second house,
  greater than the first.
The entire portal stood open before me,
  and it was built of flames of fire.

16   In every way it so excelled
  in splendor, magnificence, and extent
  that I cannot describe to you its splendor or its extent.

---

1 Compare 2Co 12:2 - *was caught up to the third heaven—whether in the body or out of the body I do not know*
2 Compare Eze 1:22 - *an expanse, shining like awe-inspiring crystal;* Exo 24:10 - *like the very heaven for clearness*

17   Its floor was *made* of fire,

above it were flashes of lightning and shooting stars,

and its ceiling was flaming fire.

18   I looked inside and saw a highly lifted throne;[1]

its appearance was as crystal,[2]

its wheels as the shining sun,[3]

and there was the sound[4] of cherubim.

19   From underneath the throne came streams of flaming fire,[5]

so that I could not look on it.

20   The Great Glory sat on it;

His clothes shined brighter than the sun

and were whiter than any snow.[6]

21   None of the angels could enter there or behold His face;[7]

because of the magnificence and glory,

no flesh could behold Him.

22   The flaming fire surrounded Him,

a great fire stood before Him,

and none around could draw close to Him.

Ten thousand times ten thousand were before Him,[8]

yet He needed no counselor.

23   The most holy ones who were close to Him

did not leave by night nor depart from Him.[9]

24   Until then I was prostrate on my face, trembling.

The Lord called me with His own mouth, saying to me,

---

1 Compare Isa 6:1 - *a throne, high and lifted up*
2 Compare Eze 1:26 - *throne, in appearance like sapphire*
3 Compare Dan 7:9, Eze 1:16 - (wheels) *appearance was like the gleaming of beryl*
4 Or *voice*; Compare Eze 1:24; 10:5 - *the sound of the wings of the cherubim*
5 Compare Dan 7:10 - *A stream of fire issued and came out from before him*
6 Compare Dan 7:9; Eze 1:28 - *clothing was white as snow; the appearance of the brightness all around*
7 Compare Isa 6:2 - *seraphim... had six wings: with two he covered his face*
8 Compare Dan 7:10; Rev 5:11 - *a thousand thousands served him, and ten thousand times ten thousand stood before him*
9 Compare Rev 4:8; Rev 7:15 - *day and night they never cease*

"Come here, Enoch, and hear My word."

25   One of the holy ones came to me and roused me.

He made me rise up and approach the door,[1]

and I bowed my face downwards.

Watchers' Wives and Offspring

15 HE SPOKE and declared to me,
        and I heard His voice,

"Do not fear, Enoch,

you righteous man and scribe of righteousness.

Approach here and hear My voice.

2   Go, say to the watchers of heaven,

who have sent you to petition for them:

'You should petition for men, and not men for you.

3   Why have you left the high, holy, and eternal heaven,

laid with women,

defiled yourselves with the daughters of men,

taken wives for yourselves,

done like the children of earth,

and fathered giants[2] *as your* sons?

4   Though you were holy, spiritual,

living the eternal life,

you defiled yourselves with the blood of women.

You have lusted *as if* with the blood of men,

and you do as they do—flesh and blood,

who die and perish.

5   Therefore I gave them wives,

that they might impregnate them,

---

1 Compare Acts 12:7, 8 - (an angel) *He struck Peter on the side and woke him*
2 Compare Num 13:33; 1Ch 20:4-8 - *Nephilim (the sons of Anak, who come from the Nephilim)*

and beget children by them,
> so they will be deprived of nothing on earth.'

6   'But you were formerly spiritual, living the eternal life,
> and immortal for all generations of the world.

7   So I have not appointed wives for you,
> because the spiritual ones of the heavens belong in
> > heaven.[1]

8   Now the giants, who are produced from the spirits and
> > *from* flesh,
> will be called demons[2] on the earth,
> and on the earth shall be their dwelling.

9   Evil spirits have come out of their bodies,
> because they are born from men;
> yet from the holy watchers is their beginning and primal
> > origin.
> They will be shades[3] on the earth,
> and they will be called demons.[4]

10   As for the spirits of heaven,
> in heaven will be their dwelling,
> but as for the demons of the earth
> > that were born on the earth,
> > on the earth will be their dwelling.

11   The spirits of the giants afflict, oppress, destroy,
> attack, do battle,[5] work destruction on the earth,
> and cause trouble.

---

1   Compare Mat 22:30; Mark 12:25; Luk 20:34-36 - *neither marry nor are given in marriage, but are like angels in heaven*

2   Or *evil spirits*; Also for *demons* in verses 9, 10, & 11

3   Or *evil spirits*

4   Compare Isa 14:9; 26:14 - *They are dead, they will not live; they are **shades**;* The word *shades* is "rapha", which is linked to a word for *giant*. The Holy Bible often linguistically connects dead spirits to giants. See Strongs H7496, 7, & 8

5   Compare Dan 10:5-6, 13 - *The prince of the kingdom of Persia*

They do not need *to eat* food, but still hunger and thirst,
    causing offenses.
These demons will rise up against the children of men
    and against the women,
      because they have come out of them.'" *1*

No Peace for the Watchers

16
  "FROM THE days of slaughter, destruction, and death of
        the giants,
the demons, having left their flesh,
    will destroy without incurring judgment *2*—
    so will they destroy until the day of the fulfillment. *3*
The great judgment,
    where the age will be fulfilled over the watchers and the godless,
    yes, it will be completely fulfilled.

2   Now as for the watchers who sent you to plead for them,
    who were previously in heaven:

3   'You were in heaven,
    but all the mysteries were not revealed to you. *4*
You knew worthless mysteries,
    and in the hardness of your hearts
you taught them to your women, *5*
    and through these mysteries
    women and men carry out great evil on the earth.'

4   Because of this, say to them, 'You have no peace.'" *6*

---

1 Compare Gen 3:14-15 - *The LORD God said to the serpent... I will put enmity
between you and the woman, and between your offspring and her offspring*
2 Compare Mar 5:7-13 - (demons) *they begged him, saying, "Send us to the pigs"...
So he (Jesus) gave them permission*
3 Compare Mat 8:29 - *Have you come here to torment us before the time?*
4 Compare 1Pe 1:12 - *things into which angels long to look*
5 Compare Amo 4:1; Eze 13:18-21
6 Compare Isa 48:22 - *"There is no peace," says the LORD, "for the wicked."*

2 ENOCH

Journeys

Enoch Shown Many Places

17 *THE ANGELS* took me,
  leading away to a certain place.
The ones there were like flaming fire,[1]
  but when they wished, they appeared as men.[2]

2 They brought me to the place of darkness,
  and to a mountain with a summit that reached to heaven.

3 I saw the places of the luminaries,
  the treasuries of the stars and of the thunder;
and *saw* into the farthest depths,
  where there was a fiery bow and arrows, their quiver,
  a flaming sword,[3] and all the lightnings.

4 They took me to the living waters,
  and to the fire of the west, that receives every setting of the sun.

5 I came to a river of fire where the fire flows like water
  and pours itself into the great sea towards the west.

6 I saw all the great rivers,
  came to the great river and to the great darkness,
  and went to the place where no flesh walks.

7 I saw the mountains of the darkness of winter

---

1 Compare Psa 104:4; Heb 1:7 - *his ministers a flaming fire*
2 Compare Heb 13:2 - *some have entertained angels unawares*
3 Compare Gen 3:24 - *fiery sword*

and the place where all the waters of the deep flow.

8   I saw the mouths of all the rivers of the earth
        and the mouth of the deep.

Winds, Pillars, and Mountains

18 I BEHELD the repositories of all the winds,
        and saw how He used them
            to order all creation and the foundations of the earth.

2   I beheld the cornerstone of the earth,
        and I saw the four winds[1] that support *both* the earth
        and the firmament of the heavens.

3   I watched how the winds stretch out the heights of the heavens,
        and have their origin between heaven and earth;
            these are the pillars of the heavens.

4   I saw the winds that turn the sky
        and cause the face of the sun and all the stars to set.

5   I watched the winds on the earth carrying the clouds.
        I beheld the paths of the angels.
    I saw, at the end of the earth,
        the firmament of the heavens above.

6   I continued and saw a place that burns day and night,
        where there are seven mountains of magnificent stones,[2]
            three towards the east, and three towards the south.

7   As for those towards the east,
        one was made of colored stone,
    one was made of pearl, and one was made of jacinth,
        and those towards the south were made of red stone.

8   But the middle one reached to heaven

---

1 Compare Rev 7:1 - *four winds*
2 Compare Eze 28:14 - *I placed you; you were on the holy mountain of God; in the midst of the stones of fire you walked.*

like the throne of God, made of alabaster,
and the summit of the throne was made of sapphire.[1]

9 And I beheld a flaming fire
that was in all the mountains.

10 I beheld a place at the end of the great earth,
at the edge of the heavens.

11 I saw a deep abyss, with columns of heavenly fire,
and among them I saw columns of fire falling.
They were beyond measure both in height and in depth.

12 Beyond that abyss, I saw a place that had no sky above,
and no ground below.[2]
There was no water upon it, and no birds,
but it was a desolate and horrible place.

13 I beheld seven stars there like great burning mountains.

When I asked about these things,
in response to me, 14 the angel said,
"This place is the end of heaven and earth;
this has become a prison for the stars and the host of heaven.

15 The stars that roll over the fire
are those who violated the commandment of the Lord at the
beginning of their rising,
because they did not come out at their appointed times.[3]

16 He was angry with them, and bound them
until the time when their guilt should be fulfilled,
even for ten thousand years."

---

1 Compare Eze 1:26, 10:1 - *a throne, in appearance like sapphire*
2 Or *a place that had no firmament of the heavens above, and no firmly founded earth beneath it.*
3 Compare Jude 1:13 - *wandering stars... gloom... has been reserved forever*

Likeness of the End

19
URIEL SAID to me, "The angels will stand here
who mingled themselves with women.

Their spirits, taking many different forms,
defile mankind and will lead them astray
into sacrificing to demons as gods. *1*

Imprisoned until the day of the great judgment
where they will be judged with finality.

2 And the wives of the fallen angels
will become sirens." *2*

3 I, Enoch, alone saw the vision, the ends of all things,
and no man will see as I have seen.

The Angels Who Watch

20
THESE ARE the names
of the holy angels who watch. *3*

2 Uriel, one of the holy angels,
who is over the world and over Tartarus. *4*

3 Raphael, one of the holy angels,
who is over the spirits of men.

4 Raguel, one of the holy angels

---

1 Compare Lev 17:7 - *their sacrifices to goat demons*; 1Co 10:20 - *what pagans sacrifice they offer to demons and not to God.*

2 Compare Zec 5:5-11 ISV - *two women coming forward with the wind filling their wings. (They had wings like those of a stork.)*; Angels are never described as female in the Holy Bible, and storks are unclean birds. These are sirens (half female, half bird). The term *sirens* is often translated as *ostrich* or *owl* in the Holy Bible: see Mic 1:8, Isa 13:21 ISV - *there owls will dwell, and goat-demons*; owls and goat demons are a strange combination, but sirens (half woman/half bird) and goat-demons (called *satyrs* in the KJV) make a more likely translation; Job 30:29 KJV - *a brother to dragons, and a companion to owls*; Isa 34:13 LXX - *habitations of monsters, and a court of ostriches*; also Jer 50:39

3 Compare Rev 8:2 - *the seven angels who stand before God*

4 Compare 2 Pet 2:4, Jude 1:6 - *Tartarus*

who takes vengeance on the world of the luminaries.[1]

5   Michael, one of the holy angels,

specifically, he that is set over the best part of mankind[2]

and over chaos.

6   Sariel, one of the holy angels,

who is set over the spirits of mankind who sin against the spirit.

7   Gabriel, one of the holy angels,

who is over paradise,[3] the serpents,[4] and the Cherubim.

8   Remiel, one of the holy angels,

whom God set over those who rise.

Desolation and the Abyss

21

I WENT to a place of chaos,

2   and I saw there something terrible:

no sky above, no earth below,

but an empty place, awful and terrible.[5]

3   There I saw seven stars of the heavens bound together in it,

like great mountains burning with fire.[6]

4   Then I said, "For what sin are they bound,

and on what account have they been cast in here?"

5   Then Uriel spoke—one of the holy angels who was with me

and was in charge of the *prisoners. He* said,

"Enoch, why do you ask,[7] and why are you eager for the truth?

6   These are among the stars of heaven,

that have violated the commandment of the Lord,

---

1 Compare Job 25:5 - *the stars are not pure in his eyes*; Jude 1:13 ISV - *They are wandering stars for whom the deepest darkness has been reserved forever*; See also Enoch 21:6

2 Compare Dan 10:21, 12:1 - Michael as the guardian of Israel

3 Compare Luk 1:19 - *I am Gabriel. I stand in the presence of God*

4 Seraphim - See Isa 6:1-2

5 Schodde translation used

6 Compare Jer 4:23-28

7 Compare Jdg 13:18 - *the angel of the LORD said to him, "Why do you ask?"*

and are bound here until ten thousand years, the time
warranted by their sins, is fulfilled." [1]

7   From there I went to another place that was still more horrible
            than the last,
      and I saw a horrible thing:
a great fire there that burned and blazed,
      and the place was split open to the end of [2] the abyss,
      filled with great descending columns of fire.
      I could not see its extent nor magnitude, nor could I imagine *it*.

8   Then I said, "How fearful is this place
            and how terrible to look at!"

9   Then Uriel, one of the holy angels who was with me, answered,
            saying, "Enoch, why do you have such fear and terror?" [3]
      I answered, "Because of this fearful place,
            and because of the spectacle of the pain."

10   And he said to me, "This place is the prison of the angels;
            they will be imprisoned here forever." [4]

The Souls of the Dead

22   THEN I went to another place,
            and he showed me in the west
            another great and high mountain of hard rock.

2   In it were four hollow places,
            deep, wide, and very smooth.
      How smooth are the hollow places
            and deep and dark to look at.

3   Then Raphael, one of the holy angels who was with me,

---

1 Compare Isa 24:21 - *the LORD will punish the host of heaven, in heaven*
2 Or - *as far as*
3 Compare Mar 4:40 - *He said to them, "Why are you so afraid?"*
4 Compare Mat 25:41 - *eternal fire prepared for the devil and his angels.*

spoke, saying,

"These hollow places have been created for this very purpose,
  that the spirits of the souls of the dead should assemble in
    them,
  yes, that all the souls of the children of men should gather
    here.

4 These places have been made to receive them
  until the day of their judgment
  and until their appointed time." [1]

5 I saw the spirits of the children of men who were dead;
  their voices reached to heaven
  and made pleas for justice. [2]

6 Then I asked Raphael,
  the watcher and holy one who was with me,
  and I said to him,
  "This spirit—whose is it whose voice goes out and makes a plea
    for justice?"

7 He answered me, saying,
  "This is the spirit that went out from Abel, [3]
  whom his brother Cain killed.
  He makes his plea for justice against him [4]
  until *Cain's* seed is destroyed from the face of the earth,
  and *until* his descendants are annihilated
  from among the seed of men."

8 Then I asked about all the hollow places,
  "Why is one separated from the other?"

9 He answered me, saying,

---

1 Laurence; truncated verse
2 Compare Rev 6:9, 10
3 Compare Heb 11:4 - *Abel... though he died, he still speaks*
4 Compare Gen 4:10; Heb 12:24

"These three *hollow places* were made
    so the spirits of the dead would be separated.
This division was made for the spirits of the righteous,
    where there is the bright spring of water.

10 This *division* was *also* made for sinners when they die,
    who are buried in the earth without judgment enacted on them
        in their lifetime.

11 Here their spirits will be set apart in this severe pain
    until the great day of judgment, punishment, and torment
of the blasphemers forever,
    and *until the great day of* retribution against their spirits;
    there He will bind them forever.

12 And this division was made for the spirits of those
    who make their suit,
who give testimony about their destruction,
    when they were killed in the days of the sinners.[1]

13 This *division* was made for the spirits of men
    who were not righteous, but were sinners,
    whose actions were evil, and their evil was made complete.
They will be *separated* with criminals like themselves,[2]
    but their spirits will not be annihilated[3] in the day of judgment
    nor will they escape from there."

14 Then I blessed the Lord of glory, saying,
    "Blessed be my Lord, the Lord of righteousness,
    who rules forever."

---

1 Compare Rev 6:10 - *avenge our blood on those who dwell on the earth*
2 Compare Luk 16:26 - *between us and you a great chasm has been fixed, in order that those who would pass from here to you may not be able, and none may cross from there to us*; Psa 1:5 ISV - *Therefore the wicked will not escape judgment, nor will sinners have a place in the assembly of the righteous.*
3 Compare Mat 25:46 - *these will go away into eternal punishment*

The Luminaries of Heaven

23 FROM THERE I went to another place
to the west of the ends of the earth.

2   I saw a burning fire that ran without resting,
    and did not pause from its course day or night,
    but *ran* regularly.

3   I asked, saying,
    "What is this that does not rest?"

4   Then Raguel,
    one of the holy angels who was with me,
    answered, saying,
"This course of fire that you have seen
    is the fire in the west
    that persecutes all the luminaries of heaven."

Seven Magnificent Mountains

24 FROM THERE, I went to another place of the earth,
and he showed me a mountain range of fire
    that burned day and night.

2   I went beyond it and saw seven magnificent mountains,
    each one unique.
Their stones were magnificent and beautiful:
    wholly magnificent, of glorious appearance, and beautiful
        exterior.
There were three towards the east, one set on the other,
    three towards the south, one upon the other,
    and deep jagged ravines, none of them joined with any other.

3   The seventh mountain was in the middle of these;
    it surpassed them in height,
resembling the seat of a throne,
    and fragrant trees surrounded the throne.

The Tree of Life

4   Among them was a tree
        such as I had never smelled,
    neither was any *other tree* among them nor any others like it.
        It had a fragrance beyond all fragrance,
    its leaves, blooms, and wood never wither forever;
        its fruit is beautiful,
        and its fruit resembles the dates of a palm.
5   Then I said,
        "How beautiful this tree is, and fragrant;
    its leaves are fair,
        and its blooms look very delightful."
6   Then Michael,
        one of the holy angels who was with me,
    and was their leader.
        answered, saying,

25 "ENOCH, WHY do you ask me about the fragrance
    of the tree,
        and why do you wish to learn the truth?"
2   Then I answered him, saying,
        "I wish to know about everything *here*,
        but especially about this tree."
3   He answered, saying,
        "This high mountain that you have seen,
    whose summit is like the throne of God,
        is His throne, where the Holy Great One,
    the Lord of Glory, the Eternal King, will sit,
        when He comes down to visit the earth with goodness.
4   As for this fragrant tree,
        no mortal is permitted to touch it[1] until the great judgment,

---

1 Compare Gen 3:22 - *Now, lest he... take also of the tree of life*

when *God* will take vengeance on all

and bring *everything* to its fulfillment forever.

This tree will then be given to the righteous and holy.[1]

5   Its fruit will be food for the chosen;[2]

it will be moved to the holy place,

to the temple of the Lord, the Eternal King.

6   Then they will rejoice with joy and be glad,

and enter into the holy place,[3]

with its fragrance in their bones.

They will live a long life on earth,[4]

such as your fathers lived in their days.

No sorrow, plague, torment, nor calamity

will touch them."[5]

7   Then I blessed the God of Glory, the Eternal King,

who has prepared such things for the righteous.

He created them and promised to give to them.

The Middle of the Earth

26 I WENT from there to the middle of the earth,[6]
and I saw a blessed place

that had trees with branches enduring and blooming

from a dismembered tree.[7]

2   There I saw a holy mountain,[8]

and underneath the mountain to the east

---

1 Compare Pro 3:13, 18 - *wisdom... a tree of life*

2 Compare Rev 2:7 - *I will grant to eat of the tree of life... in the paradise of God*

3 Compare Rev 22:14 - *have the right to the tree of life and that they may enter the city by the gates*

4 Compare Gen 3:22-24 - *take also of the tree of life and eat, and live forever*

5 Compare Rev 22:2 - *The leaves of the tree were for the healing of the nations*

6 Jerusalem; Compare Eze 38:12 - *center of the earth* - also Eze 5:5

7 Compare Joh 15:2; Rom 11:17-21 - *every branch that does bear fruit he prunes*

8 Zion

there was a stream,[1] and it flowed to the south.

3   I saw to the east a higher mountain still,[2]

and between them a deep and narrow valley;[3]

and through the valley, a stream[4] ran underneath the mountain.

4   To the west of it was another mountain,[5]

lower than the previous one and of small elevation,

and a valley deep and dry between them.

Another deep and dry valley was at the ends of the three

mountains.

5   All the valleys were deep, narrow, and of hard rock,

and trees were not planted on them.

6   I marveled at the rocks;

I marveled at the valley;

yes, I marveled very much.

Valley of the Cursed

27 THEN I said, "Why does this blessed land,

that is entirely filled with trees,

have among it this cursed valley?" [6]

2   Then Uriel,

one of the holy angels who was with me,

answered, saying,

"This cursed valley is for those who are cursed forever.

Here all the cursed will be gathered together

who speak with their lips evil words against the Lord

---

1 The brook of Siloam
2 The Mount of Olives
3 The valley of the Kedron or Jehoshaphat
4 The brook of Kedron
5 The Mount of Offence (Mount of Corruption); See 2Ki 23:13
6 The valley of Hinnom or Gehenna - Commonly translated as "hell" when used by Jesus in the New Testament. See Mat 5:22; 29, 30; Mat 10:28; Mat 18:9; Mat 23:15, 33; Mar 9:43-48; Luk 12:5; Jas 3:6

and speak harshly about His glory.[1]

Here they will be gathered together,
  and here will be their place of judgment.

3 In the last days, there will be on them
  the display of righteous judgment
  in the presence of the righteous forever;[2]
  here will the merciful bless the Lord of glory, the Eternal King.

4 In the days of judgment over the cursed,
  the righteous will bless Him for His mercy,
  in agreement with how He assigned them their fate."

5 Then I blessed the Lord of Glory,
  expressed His glory,
  and praised Him gloriously.

A Stream in the Wilderness

28 THEN I went to the east,
  into the middle of the mountain range of the desert.
I saw a wilderness *there*,[3]
  and it was solitary, full of trees and plants.

2 Water gushed out from above,
3   rushing like an abundant stream
  that flowed towards the northwest,
It caused clouds and dew
  to rise on every side.

---

1 Compare Jude 1:15 - *all the harsh things that ungodly sinners have spoken against him*
2 Compare Psa 91:8 ISV - *observe it with your eyes, and you will see how the wicked are paid back*
3 Possibly the plain of the Jordan and the rocky region separating it from Jerusalem. According to Ezek. 47:8, 12 this desert should one day be well watered and covered with trees.

Sweet-Smelling Trees

29 THEN I went to another place in the desert,
and approached to the east of this mountain range.

2   There I saw aromatic trees
      releasing the fragrance of frankincense and myrrh,
    and the trees also
      were similar to the almond tree.

A Fragrant Valley

30 BEYOND THESE, I went far to the east.
I saw another place,
    a valley *full* of water.

2   In that place was a tree whose smell
      resembled fragrant trees
      such as the mastic.

3   On the sides of those valleys
      I perceived fragrant cinnamon.
    And I proceeded beyond these to the east.

Tree-Covered Mountains

31 I SAW other mountains.
Among them were groves of trees,
    and nectar flowed out from them
      that is named sarara[1] and galbanum.

2   Beyond these mountains, I saw another mountain
      to the east of the ends of the earth;
    aloe trees[2] were on it, and all the trees were full of stacte,[3]

---

1 A kind of balsam
2 Not American aloe—modern eagle wood from South-Eastern Asia, which
has a fragrant odor when burned. As rendered in Num 26:6, Pro 7:17 - *like aloes*
3 *stacte*: sweet spice the ancient Hebrews used in holy incense

being like almond-trees.
3   When they burned it,
       it smelled sweeter than any fragrant odor.

The Garden of Righteousness

32
AFTER SMELLING these fragrant odors,
       as I looked towards the north over the mountains,
    I saw seven mountains full of choice nard, fragrant trees,
                cinnamon, and pepper.
2   Then I went over the summits of the mountains,
       far towards the east of the earth,
    passed above the Red Sea,*1* went far from it,
       and passed over the angel*2* Zotiel.
3   I came to the garden of righteousness,*3*
       and beyond those trees,
       I saw many large trees growing there.
    They had a wonderful fragrance
       and were large, very beautiful, and glorious.
    Eating of the tree of knowledge,*4*
       one learns great discernment.
4   That tree is as tall as the fir,
       its leaves are like *those of* the Carob tree,
    its fruit is like the clusters of the vine, very beautiful,
       and the fragrance of the tree reaches far.
5   Then I said, "How beautiful is the tree,
       and how pleasant to look at!"

---

1 Or *Erythraean Sea* - A general name for the Arabian, Persian, and Indian seas.
2 *angel*; In Gen 3:24, cherubim guarded the way to the Garden of Eden. Both *cherubim* and *angel* are titles that describe function (cherubim usually means *guardian*, angel means *messenger*). Thus, Zotiel could potentially be both an angel and a cherubim.
3 The garden of Eden. See Gen 2:8; Eze 28:13, 14 - *Eden... the holy mountain*
4 Or *wisdom*; the same for *knowledge* in verse 6

6   Then Raphael,
            the holy angel who was with me,
            answered, saying,
        "This is the tree of knowledge,
            of which your father of old and your mother of old,
            who were before you, have eaten.
        They learned discernment,
            their eyes were opened,
        they knew that they were naked,
            and they were driven out of the garden." [1]

The Ends of the Earth

33 FROM THERE I went to the ends of the earth
        and saw great beasts there, each one unique.
        I also saw birds of unique appearance, beauty, and voice,
            each one different from the other.
2   To the east of those beasts,
            I saw the ends of the earth where the sky meets the horizon,
            and *where* the windows of the heavens open.
3   I saw how the celestial stars come out.
        I numbered them as they came out of their openings,
            and wrote them all down.
        Each star *was recorded* one by one
            according to its number, its name, its course, its position,
                    its time, and its months,
            as Uriel, the holy angel who was with me, showed me.
4   He showed all things to me
            and wrote them down for me.
        Also, he wrote their names for me,
            and their laws and their functions. [2]

---

1 Compare Gen 3:6,7, 23
2 Or *companies* or *companions*

The Northern Winds

34

FROM THERE I went towards the north
to the ends of the earth,
and there I saw a great and glorious wonder[1]
at the ends of the whole earth.

2   Here, I saw three windows of heaven
open in the heavens.
North winds blow from each of them.
When they blow there is cold, hail, frost, snow, dew, and mist.

3   Out of one opening, they blow for good,
but when they blow through the other two openings,
they blow with violence,
and there is affliction on the earth.[2]

Windows in the West

35

FROM THERE I went towards the west
to the ends of the earth.
I saw in that place three open windows in the heavens
like I saw in the *north*,[3]
the same number of windows
and the same number of openings.

The South and the East

36

FROM THERE I went to the south
to the ends of the earth.
I saw in that place three open windows in the heavens.
From that place comes dew, mist, and wind.

---

1 Or *device*; Charles notes that *device* should read as *wonder*.
2 Or *it is with violence and affliction on the earth, and they blow with violence*.
3 Or *east*. Corruption in text. Charles notes this should read *north*.

2   From there I went to the east
      to the ends of the heavens.
    I saw three open eastern windows in the heavens
      and small openings above them.

3   The celestial stars pass through each of these small openings
      and run their course to the west
      on the path shown to them.

4   As often as I looked, I always blessed the Lord of Glory,
      and I continued to bless the Lord of Glory
    who has worked great and glorious wonders,
      to show the greatness of His work to the angels, to spirits,[1]
        and to men,
    that they might praise His work,
      praising along with all His creation;
    that they would see the might of His work,
      praise the great work of His hands,
        and bless Him forever.

---

1 Compare Eph 3:10 - *the manifold wisdom of God might now be made known to the rulers and authorities in the heavenly places*

3 ENOCH

Similitudes

37 THIS IS the second vision that he saw, the vision of wisdom that Enoch the son of Jared,[1] the son of Mahalalel, the son of Cainan, the son of Enos, the son of Seth, the son of Adam, saw.

The Vision of the Similitudes

2   This is the beginning of the words of wisdom
     that I lifted up my voice to speak,
     saying to those who live on *the* earth:
   Hear, you men of ancient times,
     and see, you that come after,
   the words of the Holy One
     that I will speak before the Lord of hosts.[2]

3   It would be better to declare *only* to the men of ancient times,
     but even for those that come after we will not withhold the
        beginning of wisdom.[3]

4   Until the present day, such wisdom has never been given[4] by
       the Lord of hosts
     as I have received according to my insight,

---

1 Genealogy - See Gen 5:1-18

2 Or *Lord of spirits*; Compare Num 27:16 - *the LORD, the God of the spirits of all flesh*; Heb 12:9 - *the Father of spirits*; Num 16:22 - *God, the God of the spirits of all flesh*; 1Sa 1:3, 4:4, 17:45 - *Lord of hosts*; so throughout Enoch *Lord of spirits* is rendered *Lord of hosts*.

3 Compare Psa 78:2, 4 - *We will not hide them... but tell to the coming generation*; Pro 9:10 - *The fear of the LORD is the beginning of wisdom, and the knowledge of the Holy One is insight.*

4 Compare 1Co 2:7 - *a secret and hidden wisdom of God*

according to the good pleasure of the Lord of hosts
   who granted my share of eternal life.[1]

5   Now three similitudes were imparted to me,
    and I lifted up my voice and told them to those that live on
        the earth.[2]

Judgment of the Wicked

38

THE FIRST similitude.
When the assembly of the godly[3] will appear,
   and sinners will be judged for their sins,
    and driven from the face of the earth,

2   when the Righteous One will appear
    before the eyes of the righteous *people*,
    whose chosen works consist in[4] the Lord of hosts.
   Light will appear to the righteous and the elect
    who dwell on the earth.
   Where will the sinners dwell then,
    and where will those who denied the Lord of hosts find refuge?
   It would be better for them if they had not been born:[5]

3   when the secrets of the righteous will be revealed,
   the sinners *are* judged,
    and the godless *are* driven from the presence of the righteous
       and elect.

4   From then on, those that possess the earth
    will no longer be powerful and exalted.
   They will be unable to see the face of the holy *ones*,

---

1 Compare Heb 11:5 - *Enoch was taken up so that he should not see death*
2 Compare Rev 14:6 - *eternal gospel to proclaim to those who dwell on earth*
3 Or *council of the holy ones*; Equivalent phrase as Psa 149:1 - *congregation of saints* in KJV
4 Or *hang on*
5 Compare Mat 26:24 - *It would have been better for that man if he had not been born*

for the Lord of hosts will cause His light to appear
on the face of the holy, righteous, and elect.

5   Then the kings and the mighty will perish
and be given into the hands
of the righteous and holy.

6   From there, none will seek mercy for themselves from the
Lord of hosts,
for their lives will be at an end.

Homes of the Righteous and of the Chosen One

39 IN THOSE days,
the chosen and holy *sons of God* [1]
descended from the high heaven,
and their seed became one with the children of men. [2]

2   And in those days, Enoch received books of zeal and wrath,
and books of anxiety and exile.
"Mercy will not be granted to them,"
says the Lord of hosts.

3   During that time, a whirlwind carried me off from the earth [3]
and set me down at the end of the heavens.

4   There I saw another vision:
the dwellings of the saints, [4]
and the resting-places of the righteous.

5   Here my eyes saw their dwellings with His righteous angels,
and their resting-places with the saints.
They petitioned, interceded,
and prayed for the children of men.

---

1 Compare Gen 6:2 - *the sons of God*
2 Compare Dan 2:43 - *they shall mingle themselves with the seed of men*
3 Compare 2Ki 2:11 - *Elijah went up by a whirlwind into heaven*
4 Or *the holy ones*; also in verse 5

Righteousness flowed before them as water,[1]
  and mercy like dew upon the earth.
So it is among them forever and ever.

6   In that place my eyes saw the Chosen One[2]
      of righteousness and of faith.
    I saw His dwelling-place
      under the wings of the Lord of hosts.[3]
    Righteousness will triumph in His days,
        and the righteous and chosen will be too many to count
      before Him forever and ever.[4]
7   All the righteous and elect before Him
      will be beautiful as fiery lights,[5]
      and their mouths will be full of blessing.
    Their lips praise the name of the Lord of hosts;
      righteousness never fails before Him;
      truth never fails in His presence.
8   I wished to stay there,
      and my spirit longed for that place,[6]
    which was prepared beforehand as my inheritance;[7]
      for this was confirmed about me
      in the presence of the Lord of hosts.[8]

---

1 Compare Amos 5:24 - *righteousness like an ever-flowing stream*
2 Compare Luke 23:34-35 - *Jesus... the Christ of God, his Chosen One!*
3 Compare Psa 91:4 - *under his wings you will find refuge*; This line was formerly the first line of verse 7
4 Compare Rev 7:9 - *that no one could number... standing before the throne and before the Lamb*
5 Compare Dan 12:3 - *those who are wise shall shine like the brightness of the sky above; and those who turn many to righteousness, like the stars forever*
6 Compare Heb 11:16 - *they desire a better country, that is, a heavenly one*
7 Compare Mat 25:34 - *inherit the kingdom prepared for you from the foundation of the world*
8 Compare Heb 11:5 - *Enoch... before he was taken he was commended as having pleased God*

9   In those days, I praised and glorified the name
        of the Lord of hosts with blessings and praises,
     because He has destined me for blessing and glory
        according to the good pleasure of the Lord of hosts.

10   For a long time my eyes regarded that place,
        and I blessed Him and praised Him, saying,
     "Blessed is He, and may He be blessed
        from the beginning and forever more."

11   Before Him there is no ceasing.
     He knows—before the world was created—what is eternal[1]
        and what will be from generation to generation.

12   Those who do not sleep: *they* bless You.[2]
     They stand before Your glory and bless, praise, and extol, saying,
     "Holy, holy, holy, is the Lord of hosts.
        He fills the earth with spirits."

13   Here my eyes saw all those who do not sleep.
        They stand before Him and bless, saying,
     "Blessed are You, and blessed be the name of the Lord
        forever and ever."

14   My face was overwhelmed,[3]
        and I could no longer look.

Four Angels

40 AFTER THAT, I saw thousands of thousands
     and ten thousand times ten thousand—[4]
     I saw a multitude beyond number and reckoning
        who stood before the Lord of hosts.

---

1 Compare Eph 1:4 - *before the foundation of the world*
2 Compare Rev 4:8 KJV - *and they rest not day and night*
3 Or *changed*; Charles notes this is not like in Exo 34:29 - *skin of his face shone*
4 Compare Rev 5:11 ISV - *They numbered 10,000's times 10,000 and thousands times thousands.*

2   On the four sides of the Lord of hosts
    I saw four presences,[1] different from those that sleep not,
and I learned their names;
    for the angel that went with me made known to me
        their names,
    and showed me all the hidden things.

3   I heard the voices of those four presences
    as they uttered praises before the Lord of glory.

4   The first voice
    blesses the Lord of hosts forever and ever.

5   The second voice
    blesses the Chosen One
    and the elect ones who trust in[2] the Lord of hosts.

6   The third voice
    prays and intercedes for those who dwell on the earth,
    and supplicates in the name of the Lord of hosts.

7   The fourth voice
    fends off the satans[3]
    and forbids them to come before the Lord of hosts to accuse
        those who live on the earth.[4]

8   After that I asked the angel of peace[5] who went with me,
    who showed me everything that is hidden,
    "Who are these four presences that I have seen,

---

1 Compare Isa 63:9 - *angel of his presence*
2 Or *lean on*
3 *satans*; In the Holy Bible, *satan* is a title for *one who stands opposed*, or *adversary*. It is not used exclusively for the devil. See Strong's Concordance. H7853
4 Compare 2Pe 2:11 - *angels... do not pronounce a blasphemous judgment against them before the Lord*; Isa 54:17 - *you shall refute every tongue that rises against you in judgment*; Note 1Ti 2:5 - *There is one mediator between God and men, the man Christ Jesus*; The word *mediator* means *reconciler*. The "fourth voice" here is not reconciling God and man, but is refuting outside accusation such as Isa 54:17.
5 *angel of peace*; Isa 33:7 - *envoys of peace*; This Isaiah verse was, according to Jerome, understood of the angels and thus could be translated as *angels of peace*. Cross reference Rosenmüller's *Scholia in loc.*

and whose words I have heard and written down?"

9   He said to me,

"The first is Michael,
the gracious and patient.*1*

The second,
who watches over the sickness and wounds
of the children of men, is Raphael.

The third,
who is set over all the powers, is Gabriel.

The fourth,
who guards the repentance unto hope *2*
of those who inherit eternal life, is named Phanuel."

10   These are the four angels of the Lord of hosts
and the four voices I heard in those days.

The Secrets of the Heavens

41 AFTER THAT, I saw all the secrets of the heavens,
how the kingdom is divided,
and how the actions of men are weighed in the balance.*3*

2   There I saw the mansions of the chosen*4*
and the mansions of the holy.

My eyes beheld all the sinners there,
those who deny the name of the Lord of hosts
being driven away, and being dragged off.*5*

They could not stay because of the punishment that goes out
from the Lord of hosts.

3   There my eyes saw the secrets of the lightning, of the thunder,

---

1 Compare Jude 1:9 - *Michael... he did not presume*
2 See verse 7 footnotes; Phanuel prevents accusers (satans) from challenging
the repentance of sinners that have inherited eternal life. See Job 1:8-12
3 Compare Job 31:6; Pro 16:2; 21:2; 24:12 - *Let me be weighed in a just balance*
4 Compare Joh 14:2 KJV - *In my Father's house are many mansions*
5 Compare Mat 7:23 - *depart from me, you workers of lawlessness*

and the secrets of the winds,[1]
how they are divided to blow across the earth,
    and the secrets of the clouds and dew.
There I witnessed where they come from
    and from what place they water the dusty earth.

4   I beheld closed chambers there
        that separate out the winds:
    the chamber of the hail and winds,[2]
        of the mist,[3] and of the clouds.
    And his cloud hovers over the earth
        from the beginning of the age.[4]

5   I saw the chambers of the sun and moon,
        where they go, how far,
        and their glorious return.
    I saw how one is superior to the other,
        their stately orbit,
        and how they do not leave their orbit.
    They add nothing to their orbit,
        and they take nothing from it.
    They keep faith with each other,
        according to the oath[5] that binds them together.

6   First the sun goes out and travels his path
        according to the commandment of the Lord of hosts,
        and mighty is His name forever and ever.

7   After that, I saw the visible and the invisible path of the moon;
        there she runs her set path by day and by night—
    the one *great light* holding a position opposite to the other

---

1 Compare Job 38:24 ISV - *Where is the lightning diffused or the east wind scattered around the earth?*
2 Compare Job 38:22 - *the storehouses of the hail*
3 Compare Gen 2:5-6 - *the LORD God had not caused it to rain... a mist was going up from the land and was watering the whole face of the ground*
4 Possible reference to either Gen 1:2 or 2:6.
5 *the oath*; See Enoch 69:13

before the Lord of hosts.

They give thanks, praise, and do not rest,
   because to them, praising is rest.

8   For the sun changes often
      for a blessing or a curse.

The course of the path of the moon
      is light to the righteous and darkness to the sinners

in the name of the Lord, who made a separation
      between the light and the darkness,

divided the spirits of men,[1]
      and strengthened the spirits of the righteous,
      in the name of His righteousness.

9   For no angel hinders, and no power is able to hinder;[2]
      for the Judge sees them all,
      and He judges them all in His presence.

Wisdom and Iniquity Find Homes

42 WISDOM FOUND no place where she could stay.
Then a dwelling-place was assigned to her in the heavens.[3]

2   Wisdom went out to make her dwelling
      among the children of men,
      and found no place to stay.[4]

Wisdom returned to her place,
      and took her seat among the angels.[5]

3   Iniquity went out from her chambers;

---

1 Compare Mat 25:32, 33 - *he will separate people one from another*
2 Compare Rom 8:38-39 - *I am sure that neither... angels... nor powers... will be able to separate us from the love of God in Christ Jesus our Lord.*
3 Compare Job 28:20-24 ISV- *wisdom... understanding... he knows where they live.*
4 See Proverbs 1:20-25
5 Compare Job 28:12-13 ISV - *Where can wisdom be found? Where is understanding's home? Mankind doesn't appreciate their value; and you won't find it anywhere on earth.*

whom she did not look for, she found,
and stayed with them,
as mist in a desert and dew on a thirsty land.

Parable of the Saints

43 I SAW other lightnings and the stars of the heavens.
I saw how He called them all by their names,[1]
and they listened to Him.

2 I saw how they were weighed on the scales of justice,
according to their light, to the width of their places,
the day of their appearance, and their course.
One flash of lightning produced another,
and in number they were as many as the angels,
and they were loyal to each other.

3 I asked the angel,
the one who went with me to reveal these secrets,
"What are these?"

4 He said to me,
"The Lord of hosts has shown you these as a parable.[2]
These are the names of the holy who live on the earth
and believe in the name of the Lord of hosts forever and ever."

Stars and Lightning

44 ANOTHER THING I saw
about the lightning:
how some of the stars arise
and become shooting stars[3]
and cannot part with their new form.

---

1 Compare Psa 147:4; Isa 40:26 - *stars... calling them all by name*
2 lit. *their parable*
3 Or *lightnings*

The Second Similitude

45

THIS IS the second similitude
about those who reject the heavenly city
and deny the name of the Lord of the spirits.

2   They will not rise to heaven
and will not move on the earth.
Such will be the fate of the sinners
who have denied the name of the Lord of hosts,
who are kept for the day of suffering and tribulation.

3   "On that day, My Chosen One will sit on the throne of glory,
He will test their works,
and they will have *many* places of rest beyond number.
Their souls will grow strong within them
when they see My Chosen One,
and *see* those who call on My glorious name.
4   Then I will send My Chosen One to live among them.[1]
I will transform heaven[2]
and make it an eternal blessing and *eternal* light;
5   I will transform the earth and make it a blessing,[3]
and I will cause My chosen to live there,[4]
but the sinners and evil-doers will not set foot on it."

6   "I will satisfy My righteous ones with peace,
bringing them into My presence,
but the condemnation of sinners will draw near,
that I may destroy them from the face of the earth."

---

1 Compare Joh 1:14 - *the Word became flesh and dwelt among us... the only Son from the Father*
2 Compare Isa 65:17 - *I create new heavens and a new earth*
3 Compare Rev 21:1 - *a new heaven and a new earth*
4 Compare Isa 66:22 - *new heavens and the new earth... so shall your offspring... remain*

The Ancient of Days and the Son of Man

46
THERE I saw the Ancient of Days,[1]
and His head was white like wool.
Another was with Him,
> whose face had the appearance of a man,
and His face was full of grace,
> like one of the holy angels.[2]

2 I asked the angel who went with me
> and showed me all the hidden things,
about that Son of Man,[3]
> who He was, where He was from,
> and why He went with the Ancient of Days.

3 He answered, saying to me,
> "This is the Son of Man who has righteousness,
> and righteousness stays with Him.[4]
He reveals the treasures of the hidden things,[5]
> because the Lord of hosts has chosen Him,
and His inheritance has surpassed all
> before the Lord of hosts in eternal truth.

4 This Son of Man that you have seen
> will raise up the kings and the mighty from their seats,[6]
the strong from their thrones,
> loosen the reins of the strong,
> and break the teeth of the sinners.[7]

---

1 Or *one who had a head of days*. Compare Dan 7:13
2 Compare Act 6:15 - *(Stephen) his face was like the face of an angel*
3 The Messiah; used in the same sense as Dan 7:13-14; Luk 18:31; in total, 81 occurrences in the gospels of the New Testament, all referring to Jesus.
4 Compare Jer 23:5 - *justice and righteousness*
5 Compare Isa 11:3-5 - *He shall not judge by what his eyes see, or decide disputes by what his ears hear*; Pro 25:2 - *It is the glory of God to conceal things, but the glory of kings is to search things out*; Col 2:2-3 - *Christ, in whom are hidden all the treasures of wisdom and knowledge.*
6 Compare Isa 49:7 - *Kings shall see and arise*
7 Compare Psa 3:7; 58:6 - *you break the teeth of the wicked*

5 He will topple kings from their thrones and their dominions,
because they do not exalt and praise Him,
nor humbly acknowledge the authority
that bestowed their kingdom.
6 He will strike the composure of the strong,
and will fill them with shame.
They will dwell in darkness,
and worms will be their beds.[1]
They will have no hope of rising from their beds,
because they do not exalt the name of the Lord of hosts.
7 These are the ones who cast down the stars of heaven,[2]
raise their hands against the Most High,
and tread into the earth those who dwell upon it.[3]
All their deeds manifest unrighteousness,
their power rests upon their riches,
their faith is in the gods they made with their hands,
and they deny the name of the Lord of hosts.
8 They persecute the temples where His people gather
and the faithful who cling to the name of the Lord of hosts."

The Prayer of the Righteous

47 IN THOSE days,
the prayer of the righteous will rise,[4]
and the blood of the righteous *will rise* from the earth
before the Lord of hosts.
2 In those days, the holy ones
who dwell above in the heavens
will unite with one voice,

---

1 Compare Mar 9:47-48 - hell, 'where their worm does not die'
2 Or *who judge the stars of heaven;* See Enoch 43:4
3 Compare Dan 8:10 - *the stars it threw down to the ground and trampled*
4 Compare Rev 8:4 - *prayers of the saints, rose before God*

supplicate, pray,
magnify, and give thanks,
   blessing the name of the Lord of hosts,
on account of the blood of the righteous that has been shed;
   that the prayer of the righteous may not be in vain[1] before the
      Lord of hosts;
that judgment may be done to them,
   and that His patience may not endure forever.

3   In those days, I saw the Ancient of Days
   when He seated himself on the throne of His glory,
   and the books of the living were opened before Him.[2]
All His hosts in heaven above and His counselors
   stood before him.

4   The hearts of the holy were filled with joy,
   because the number of the righteous had been offered,[3]
and the prayer of the righteous had been heard,
   and *vengeance for* the blood of the righteous
   had been required before the Lord of hosts.

The Fountain of Righteousness and the Fate of Many

48 IN THAT place, I saw the fountain of righteousness that was
      inexhaustible.[4]
Around it were many fountains of wisdom.
All the thirsty drank of them
   and were filled with wisdom.
Their dwellings were with the righteous, holy, and elect.

2   In that hour the Son of Man[5] was named

---

1 Compare Rev 6:10 - *how long before you will judge and avenge our blood*
2 Compare Exo 32:32; Psa 69:28; Dan 12:1; Rev 20:12 - *book of the living*
3 Compare Rev 7:4-9
4 Compare Isa 55:1 ISV - *Come, everyone who is thirsty, come to the waters!*
5 The Messiah; used in the same sense as Dan 7:13-14; Luk 18:31; in total, 81 occurrences in the gospels of the New Testament, all referring to Jesus.

in the presence of the Lord of hosts,

and His name *was declared* before the Ancient of Days.[1]

3   Yes, before the sun and the signs[2] were created,[3]

before the stars of the heavens were made,

His name was named before the Lord of hosts.[4]

4   He will be a staff to the righteous

to lean on and not fall.

He will be the light of the nations,[5]

the hope of those who are troubled in heart.[6]

5   All who dwell on the earth

will fall down and worship before Him,[7]

will praise, and bless,

and celebrate with song the Lord of hosts.

6   For this reason, He has been chosen

and hidden in the presence of *the Lord*;[8]

before the foundation of the world and forever more.[9]

7   The wisdom of the Lord of hosts

has revealed Him to the holy and righteous.

For He has preserved the inheritance of the righteous,[10]

because they have hated and despised this world of

unrighteousness,[11]

and have hated all its works and ways

in the name of the Lord of hosts.

---

1 Or *one who had a head of days.* Compare Dan 7:13

2 *signs*, meaning constellations of the zodiac; Job 38:32 ISV - *constellations*

3 Compare Mic 5:2 - *whose coming forth is from of old, from ancient days*

4 Compare Joh 1:1-4 - *He was in the beginning with God... All things were made through him*

5 Or *Gentiles*; Compare Luk 2:32; Isa 42:6; 49:6 - *a light for the nations*

6 Compare Isa 61:1-2 - *to bind up the brokenhearted*

7 Compare Php 2:10 - *at the name of Jesus every knee should bow*

8 Compare Isa 49:2 - *in the shadow of his hand he hid me* (Jesus)

9 Compare 1Pe 1:19-20; Rev 13:8 - *before the foundation of the world*

10 Compare Tit 1:1-2 - *hope of eternal life... promised before the ages began*

11 Compare Eze 9:4-6

For in His name, *the name of the Son of Man*, they are saved,[1]
and according to His good pleasure,
their lives have been redeemed.

8   In these days, the kings of the earth
will be ashamed,
along with the strong who possess the land
by the works of their hands.
For on the day of their anguish and affliction
they will not *be able to* save themselves.

Judgment of the Wicked

9   "I will give them over
into the hands of my chosen.
As straw in the fire,
so will they burn[2]
in the presence of the holy.
As lead in the water,
they will sink [3]
in the presence of the righteous.
No trace of them
will be found again.

10   On the day of their afflictions,
there will be rest on the earth."

Before Him they will fall
and will not rise again.[4]
There will be no one

---

1 Compare 1Co 6:11 ISV - *you were justified in the name of our Lord Jesus the Messiah and by the Spirit of our God;* Acts 4:12 - *there is no other name... by which we must be saved*
2 Compare Rev 20:14 - *Death and Hades were thrown into the lake of fire*
3 Compare Exo 15:10 ISV - *they sank like lead in the mighty waters*
4 Compare Psa 36:12 - *the evildoers lie fallen; they are thrust down, unable to rise*

> to lend a hand to lift them up,
> because they denied the Lord of hosts
>   and His Anointed.*[1]*
> The name of the Lord of hosts be blessed!

Power and Wisdom of the Chosen One

49 FOR WISDOM is poured out like water,
and glory endures before Him forever more.

2   For He is mighty in all the secrets of righteousness.
Unrighteousness shall disappear as a shadow,
   and will not continue;
      because the Chosen One stands before the Lord of hosts.
His glory is forever and ever,
   and His might unto all generations.

3   In Him dwells the spirit of wisdom,
      the spirit that gives insight,
the spirit of understanding and of might,
   and the spirit of those who have fallen asleep in righteousness.

4   He will judge the secret things,*[2]*
      and none will be able to utter a lying word before Him;
for He is the Chosen One before the Lord of hosts according to
         His good pleasure.

Repentance of the Nations

50 IN THOSE days a change will take place
for the holy and elect.

The light of *many* days will rest on them,
   and glory and honor will come to the holy *ones*.

---

1 Compare Psa 2:2 - *against the LORD and against his Anointed;* Also Mat 10:33
2 Compare Isa 11:3-4 - *He shall not judge by what his eyes see, or decide disputes by what his ears hear, but with righteousness*

2   On the day of affliction,

       evil will gather over the sinners,

    but the righteous will be victorious

       in the name of the Lord of hosts.

    He will cause the nations[1] to see it

       that they may repent[2]

    and turn from the works of their hands.

3   Though they had no honor through the name of the Lord of
         hosts,

       yet through His name they will be saved.

    The Lord of hosts will have compassion on them,

       for His compassion is great,

4   and He is righteous in judgment.

    In the presence of His glory,

       unrighteousness will cease.

    At His judgment, the unrepentant will perish before Him.

5   "From then on, I will have no mercy on them,"

       says the Lord of hosts.

Separation of the Dead

51

1   "IN THOSE days the earth will give back
what has been entrusted to it.

    Sheol will give back what it has received,

       and hell will give back what it owes.[3]

    For in those days the Chosen One will arise;

2   He will choose the righteous and holy from among them,

       for the day of their salvation is near.

3   The Chosen One will in those days sit on My throne,

---

1 Or *the others*

2 Compare Zec 8:23 ISV - *Let us go up to Jerusalem with you, because we heard that God is with you*

3 Compare Rev 20:13 - *Death and Hades gave up the dead who were in them*

and His mouth will pour forth all the secrets of wisdom
and counsel.
For the Lord of hosts has given *all this* to Him and has
glorified Him.[1]

4   In those days the mountains will leap like rams,
and the hills will skip like lambs satisfied with milk.
The faces of the angels in heaven will brighten with joy.

5   The earth will rejoice;
the righteous will dwell on it;
the chosen will walk on it."

Fate of the Seven Metal Mountains

52

AFTER THOSE days in that place
where I saw the visions of what is hidden—
for I had been carried off in a whirlwind,[2]
and it carried me towards the west—

2   there my eyes saw the secret things of heaven
that will take place:
a mountain of iron and a mountain of copper,
a mountain of silver and a mountain of gold,
a mountain of soft metal and a mountain of lead.

3   I asked the angel who went with me, saying,
"What are these things that I have seen in secret?"

4   He said to me,
"All these things that you have seen
will serve the dominion of his Anointed
that He may be potent and mighty on the earth."

5   Also, the angel of peace answered, saying to me,
"Wait a little, and you will be shown
the secret things that surround the Lord of hosts.

---

1 Compare 1Co 2:7, 8
2 Compare 2Ki 2:11 - *Elijah went up by a whirlwind into heaven*

6   These mountains that your eyes have seen,
         the mountain of iron, the mountain of copper,
     the mountain of silver, the mountain of gold,
         the mountain of soft metal, and the mountain of lead,
     all these will be in the presence of the Chosen One
         as wax before the fire,
     and *melt* like the water that streams down from above,
         and they will become powerless before His feet.
7   It will come to pass in those days that none will be saved,
         neither by gold nor by silver,
         and none will be able to escape.
8   There will be no iron for war,
         nor will anyone wear a breastplate.
     Bronze will be of no service;
         tin will not be valued;
         lead will not be desired.
9   All these things will be rejected and destroyed
         from the surface of the earth,
     when the Chosen One appears
         in the presence of the Lord of hosts."

The Valley of Jehoshaphat

53 THERE MY eyes saw a deep valley with open mouths.
     All who dwell on the earth, sea, and islands
     will bring gifts, presents, and tokens of homage,
         but that deep valley will not become full.[1]
2   Their hands commit lawless deeds,
         and the sinners devour all whom they lawlessly oppress.

_____

1 Compare Joel 3:2 - *I will gather all the nations and bring them down to the Valley of Jehoshaphat. And I will enter into judgment with them there, on behalf of my people and my heritage Israel*

The sinners will be destroyed
   in the presence of the Lord of hosts.
They will be banished from the face of His earth,
   and they will perish forever and ever.

3   For I saw all the angels of punishment
   going and preparing all the chains of the accusers.

4   I asked the angel of peace who went with me,
   "For whom are they preparing these chains?"

5   He said to me,
   "They are preparing these for the kings and the mighty of this
      earth to bring about their end.

6   After this the Righteous and Chosen One
   will cause the house of His congregation to appear,
   forever unchanging in the name of the Lord of hosts.

7   These mountains will not stand firm before His righteousness,
   and the hills will be as fountains of water,
   and the righteous will have rest from the oppression of sinners."

Judgment on the Hosts of Azazel

54   I LOOKED and turned to another part of the earth,
   and saw there a deep valley with burning fire.

2   *The angels of punishment* brought the kings and the mighty,
   and cast them into this deep valley.

3   There my eyes saw how they made their instruments,
   iron chains of immeasurable weight.

4   I asked the angel of peace who went with me, saying,
   "Who are these chains being prepared for?"

5   He said to me,
   "These are being prepared for the hosts of Azazel,
so that *the angels of punishment* can take them and cast them
   into the abyss of complete condemnation,

and they will cover the jaws *of the abyss* with rough stones
    as the Lord of hosts commanded.

6   Michael, Gabriel, Raphael, and Phanuel
    will take hold of them on that great day.
    They will cast them on that day into the burning furnace,
    so the Lord of hosts can take vengeance on them
for their unrighteousness in becoming servants of Satan
    and leading astray those who live on the earth."

The Great Flood

7   "In those days, punishment will come from the Lord of hosts,
    and He will open all the chambers of waters that are above
        the heavens,
    and of the fountains that are beneath the earth.[1]

8   All the waters will be joined with the waters:[2]
    that which is above the heavens is the masculine,
    and the water that is beneath the earth is the feminine.

9   They will destroy all who live on the earth
    and those who live under the ends of the heavens.

10   Because of this they will recognize their unrighteousness
    that they have worked on the earth,
    and they will perish by these *waters*."

The First Judgment and the Final Judgment

55 AFTER THAT the Ancient of Days[3] repented, saying,
"In vain, I have destroyed all who live on the earth." [4]

2   He swore by His great name,

---

1 Compare Gen 7:11 - *the fountains of the great deep burst forth, and the windows of the heavens were opened*

2 Compare Gen 1:6-7 - *separate the waters from the waters*

3 Or *Head of Days*

4 Compare Jer 2:30 - *In vain have I struck your children; they took no correction*

"From now on, I will not do this to all who live on the earth,[1]
and I will set a sign in the heavens.[2]
This will be a pledge of good faith between Me and them forever,
so long as heaven is above the earth."

Judgment of the End Times

3 "In the latter *days*, according to My command,
when I desire to overpower them by the hand of the angels
on the day of tribulation and pain,
I will cause My punishment and My wrath to stay on them,
says God, the Lord of hosts.
4 You kings and mighty who dwell on the earth,
you will behold my Chosen One,
how He sits on the throne of glory and judges Azazel
along with all his associates and all his hosts
in the name of the Lord of hosts."

Angels and Demons Who Sinned

56 I SAW there the hosts of angels marching
who carried out punishment;
they held scourges and chains of iron and bronze.
2 I asked the angel of peace who went with me, saying,
"To whom are these who hold the scourges going?"
3 He said to me,
"To the watchers and the demons,[3]
to cast them into the deep abyss of the valley.

---

1 Compare Gen 9:11 - *never again shall there be a flood to destroy the earth*
2 Compare Gen 9:13-17 - *I have set my bow in the cloud, and it shall be a sign of the covenant between me and the earth.*
3 Or *their chosen and beloved ones*; Substitution per Charles' notes. So in verse 4.

4   Then that valley will be filled
      with the watchers and the demons.
    The days of their lives will be at an end,
      and their days of leading *others* astray
    will not be tallied from then on."

Last Struggle of Heathen Powers Against Israel

5   "In those days the angels will return
      and hurl themselves to the east
      upon the Parthians and Medes.
    They will stir up the kings,
      so that a spirit of unrest will come on them,
    and rouse them from their thrones,
      that they may break forth as lions from their lairs,
      and as hungry wolves among their flocks.[1]

6   They will go up and trample
      the land of His chosen ones,
    and in their path, the land of His chosen ones
      will become a threshing floor and a highway.

7   But the city of my righteous
      will be a hindrance to their horses.
    They will begin to fight among themselves.
    Their right hands will be strong against themselves,
      and a man will not know his brother,
    nor a son his father or his mother,
      until the corpses from their slaughter are without number,
      and their punishment is not in vain.

8   In those days Sheol will open its jaws,
      will swallow them up,
      and their destruction will be at an end.

---

1 Compare Eze 38:14-17 - *In the latter days I will bring you against my land*

Sheol will devour the sinners
   in the presence of the chosen."

A Host of Coming Chariots

57
IT HAPPENED after this
   that I saw another host of chariots,
 and men riding on them,
   coming on the winds from the East,
   and from the Southwest.

2   The noise of their chariots rumbled,
   and when this turmoil took place,
the holy ones from heaven remarked on it,
   and the pillars of the earth were shaken from their places.
The sound of *the chariots* was heard from one end
      of heaven to the other simultaneously,

3   and they all fell down and worshiped the Lord of hosts.

This is the end of the second similitude.

The Third Similitude

58
I BEGAN to speak the third similitude
   about the righteous and elect:

2   Blessed are you, the righteous and chosen,
   for glorious is your inheritance.

3   The righteous will be in the light of the sun.
   and the chosen in the light of eternal life.
The days of their lives will be unending,
   and the days of the holy without number.

4   They will seek the light
   and find righteousness with the Lord of hosts.
There will be peace to the righteous

in the name of the Eternal Lord.

5   After this it will be said to the holy *ones* in heaven
     that they should seek out the secrets of righteousness,
the heritage of faith,
     "For it has become bright as the sun upon earth,
     and the darkness is past." [1]

6   There will be a light that never ends,
     and no limit to their days.
For the darkness will first be destroyed,
     and the light established before the Lord of hosts.
The light of uprightness *will be* established forever
     before the Lord of hosts.

The Lights and the Thunder

59   IN THOSE days my eyes saw the secrets of the
     lightnings, the lights,
and the judgments they execute. [2]
They brighten for a blessing or a curse
     as the Lord of hosts decides. [3]

2   There I saw the secrets of the thunder,
     and how when it resounds above in the heavens,
     the sound of it is heard.
He caused me to see the judgments executed on the earth,
     whether they be for well-being and blessing, or for a curse
     according to the word of the Lord of hosts.

3   After that, all the secrets of the lights and lightnings
     were shown to me.
They brighten for blessing and for satisfying.

---

1 Compare 1Jn 1:5 KJV - *God is light, and in him is no darkness at all.*
2 lit. *their judgment*
3 Compare Job 36:30, 31 - *scatters his lightning... by these he judges peoples; he gives... abundance.*

4 ENOCH

Noah

Noah Has a Vision

60 IN THE year five hundred, in the seventh month, on the fourteenth day of the month,[1] in the life of *Noah*.[2] In a vision, I saw how a mighty quaking made the heaven of heavens shake. The host of the Most High, and the angels, a thousand thousands and ten thousand times ten thousand, were unsettled from a great upheaval.

2   The Ancient of Days[3] sat on the throne of His glory,
          and the angels and the righteous stood around Him.

3   A great trembling seized me;
          fear took hold of me;
          my loins gave way.
       I lost all composure,[4]
          and I fell on my face.

4   Michael sent an angel from among the holy ones
          to set me on my feet.
       When he straightened me,[5] my spirit returned,
          for I had been unable to endure the look of this host,
          the commotion, and the quaking of the heavens.

---

1 Eve of the Feast of Tabernacles
2 The manuscripts read *Enoch*. However, this date is drawn from Gen 5:32, and is a date in the life of Noah and not Enoch. The translators were in agreement. For *Enoch* we should read *Noah*.
3 Or *Head of Days*
4 Or *dissolved were my reins*
5 Or *and when he had raised me up*; Also for *set me on my feet*

5   Michael said to me:

"Why are you unsettled by this vision?
> Until today, the day of His mercy remained.

He has been merciful and patient
> to those who live on the earth.

6   When that day and the power, the punishment,
>> and the judgment come,
> that the Lord of hosts prepared for those
> who bow to the righteous law, and *yet* deny the righteous
>> judgment—[1]

that day is prepared for those
> who take His name in vain:[2]

for the elect a day of covenant,
> but for sinners an interrogation.

25 [3] When the punishment of the Lord of hosts rests on
>> them,
> it will rest so that the punishment of the Lord of hosts
>> may not come in vain,

and it will slay the children with their mothers
> and the children with their fathers.

Afterwards, the judgment will take place according to
>> His mercy and His patience."

Leviathan and Behemoth

7   On that day two monsters were separated,
> a female monster named Leviathan,[4]
> to dwell in the abyss of the ocean over the fountains of

---

1 Compare Mat 23:23 - *hypocrites! For you tithe... and have neglected the weightier matters of the law: justice and mercy and faithfulness.*
2 Compare Exo 20:7 - *You shall not take the name of the LORD your God in vain*
3 The translators struggled with the order of verses in this chapter.
4 Job 41 describes Leviathan as masculine.

the waters.

8 But the male is named Behemoth;

he lays his breast in a desert wilderness

in the land of Nod, to the east of Eden,[1] where the elect
and righteous dwell,

where my great-grandfather was taken up, the seventh
from Adam,

the first man the Lord of hosts created.

9 I implored the other angel

that he should show me the might of those monsters,

how they were parted in one day and sent away,

the one into the abyss of the sea,

and the other to the desert wilderness.

10 He said to me, "Mortal man,[2] on this *subject* you

seek to know hidden things."

24[3] The angel of peace who was with me said,

"These two monsters, prepared according to the

greatness of God, will be food for *the just*." [4]

Noah Shown the Elements

11 Then another angel went with me and showed me
what was hidden.

He told me what is first and last in the heavens above,

in the depths of the earth, at the ends of the heavens,

and on the foundation of the heavens.

12 *The angel told me about* the chambers of the winds,

---

1 Gen 4:16 - Nod, east of Eden

2 Or *son of man* or *human being*; As in Eze 2:1

3 Verse order uncertain

4 End of line missing. Reconstructed with *the just* by Charles. According to
other apocryphal and rabbinical writings these two monsters are to be the food
of the just in the Messianic times.

how the winds are divided, how they are weighed,
and *how* the portals of the winds are reckoned,
     each according to the power of the wind, the power of
          the lights of the moon,
according to the power that is fitting:
     the divisions of the stars according to their names,
     and how all the divisions are divided.

13 Peals of thunder *are divided* based on where
          they fall,
     and the divisions of the lighting allow them to flash,[1]
     so their host can immediately obey.[2]

14 For the thunder has places of rest assigned
     while it waits for its reverberation.
The thunder and lightning are inseparable.
Although *they are* not one and undivided,
     they both go together through the spirit and do not separate.

15 For when the lightning flashes, the thunder utters its voice,
     and the spirit enforces a pause during the peal, and divides
          equally between them;
     for the treasury of their peals is like the sand.
Each one of them as it peals is held in with a bridle,
     turned back by the power of the spirit,
     and pushed forward according to the many quarters
          of the earth.

16 The spirit of the sea is potent[3] and strong,
     and according to the might of his strength he draws *the sea*
          back with a rein.
So it is driven forward and disperses across all the
          mountains of the earth.

17 The frost has an assigned angel of its own,

---

1 Or *divisions that are made among the lightnings that it may lighten*
2 Compare Job 28:26 - *a way for the lightning of the thunder*
3 Or *masculine*

and the angel over the hail is good.

18   The spirit of the snow leaves his chambers when he is strong;
the spirit inside is special,
what rises from it is like smoke,
and its name is frost.*1*

19   The spirit of the mist is not mixed with them
in their chambers,
but it has a special chamber,
for its course is glorious*2* both in light and in darkness,
in winter and in summer,
and inside its chamber is an angel.

20   The spirit of the dew has its dwelling at the ends
of the heavens,
is connected with the chambers of the mist,
and its course is in winter and summer.
Its clouds and the clouds of the mist are connected,
and the one gives to the other.

21   When the spirit of the mist leaves its chamber,
the angels come, open the chamber, and lead it out.*3*
When it scatters over the whole earth,
it unites with the water on the earth.
And whenever it unites with the water on the earth . . . *4*

22   For the waters are for those who dwell on the earth;
for they are nourishment for the earth from the Most High
who is in heaven.
Therefore, mist has regulated amounts,
and the angels receive it.

23   These things I saw towards the Garden of the Righteous.

---

1 Compare Job 37:10 - *By the breath of God ice is given*
2 Or *oppressive*
3 Compare Job 37:11, 12 - *turn around and around by his guidance*
4 Line missing in the text

The Measures of the Righteous

61

I SAW in those days how long cords were given to those angels, and they lifted high*¹* and went to the north.

2   I asked the angel, saying to him,

"Why have those *angels* taken these cords and left?"

He said to me,

"They have gone to measure." *²*

3   Then the angel who went with me said,

"These will return with the measures of the righteous,

and the boundaries of righteousness to the righteous,

that they may rest in the name of the Lord of hosts,

forever and ever.*³*

4   The chosen will from then on live with the chosen;

those measures are given for strict observance,*⁴*

and they will strengthen righteousness.

5   These measures will expose all the secrets of the depths of

the earth:*⁵*

those who were destroyed by the desert,

devoured by the beasts,

and devoured by the fish of the sea.

They will return and trust in the day of the Chosen One;

for none will die in the presence of the Lord of hosts,*⁶*

nor will any be capable of dying." *⁷*

6   All who dwell above in the heavens received a command,

power, one voice, and one light that was like fire.

7   First, with their voices, they blessed him;

---

1 Or *took wing and flew*; Schodde notes that *took wing* was added to the text.
2 Compare Eze 40:3, 6 - *a measuring reed in his hand... measured the threshold*
3 Compare Zec 2:1-5 - *To measure Jerusalem... its width and what is its length*
4 Or *for faith*
5 Compare Rev 20:13 - *Death and Hades gave up the dead who were in them*
6 Compare Rom 8:38-39
7 Or *none can be destroyed*

they exalted him; they glorified him with wisdom.
They were wise in words and in the spirit of life.

8   The Lord of hosts placed the Chosen One on the throne
          of glory.
He will judge all the works of the holy, in heaven above,
     and weigh their deeds in the balance.

9   He will lift up His face to judge their secret ways
          according to the word of the name of the Lord of hosts,
     and their paths according to the way of the righteous
          judgment of the Lord of hosts.
Then, with one voice, they will all speak, bless,
     glorify, extol, and sanctify
     the name of the Lord of hosts.

10   He will summon all the hosts of the heavens,
          and all the holy ones above:
the hosts of God, the cherubim, seraphim, ophanim,[1]
     all the angels of power, all the angels of principalities,[2]
the Chosen One,
     and the other Power on the earth over the water on that day.[3]

11   They will raise one voice,
          and will bless, glorify, and exalt in the spirit of faith,
in the spirit of wisdom, in the spirit of patience,
     in the spirit of mercy, in the spirit of judgment,
     in the spirit of peace, and in the spirit of goodness.[4]
All will say with one voice, "Blessed is He,
     and may the name of the Lord of hosts be blessed
          forever and ever."

12   All those that never sleep, high in the heavens, will bless Him.
All his holy ones, who are in heaven, will bless Him,

---

1 Hebrew word for *wheel* used in Eze 1:15-21; Eze 10:2, 6, 9-13; See Dan 7:9
2 Compare Eph 6:12 KJV, Rom 8:38 KJV - *principalities... powers*
3 **The Holy Spirit.** See Gen 1:2 - *Spirit of God... over the face of the waters.*
4 Compare Rev 1:4, 3:1, 4:5, 5:6 - *seven spirits of God*

all the chosen, who dwell in the garden of life;
> every spirit of light who is able to bless, glorify, extol,
> and hallow Your blessed name.
All flesh will glorify and bless Your name beyond measure
> forever and ever.

13 For great is the mercy of the Lord of hosts,
> and He is slow to anger.
All His works, and all that He has made,
> He has revealed to the righteous and chosen,
> in the name of the Lord of hosts.

Judgment Before the Son of Man

62 SO THE Lord commanded the kings, the mighty, and the exalted,
> and those who live on the earth, saying,
"Open your eyes and lift up your horns
> if you are able to recognize the Chosen One."

2 The Lord of hosts seated Him on the throne of His glory,
> and the spirit of righteousness was poured on Him.
The word of His mouth slays all the sinners,[1]
> and all the unrighteous are destroyed at His presence.
3 These will stand up in that day: all the kings, the mighty,
> the exalted, and those who hold the earth.
They will see and recognize
> how He sits on the throne of His glory.
Righteousness is judged before Him,
> and no lying word is spoken before Him.
4 Then pain will come over them
> like a woman in childbirth

---

1 Compare 2Th 2:8 - *the Lord Jesus will kill with the breath of his mouth*

whose labor is severe,

> when her child enters the mouth of the womb,

> and she has pain in giving birth.

5   One group of them will look to the other,

> and they will be terrified.

Their faces will be dismayed,

> and pain will seize them

> when they see that Son of Man[1] sitting on the throne of

>> His glory.

6   The kings, the mighty, and all who possess the earth

> will bless, glorify, and praise Him who rules over all,

> Him who was hidden.

7   For from the beginning the Son of Man was hidden.[2]

The Most High preserved Him in the presence of His might

> and revealed Him to the chosen.[3]

8   The congregation of the chosen and holy will be founded,[4]

> and all the chosen will stand before Him on that day.

9   All the kings, the mighty, the exalted,

> and those who rule the earth

> will fall down before Him on their faces and worship.

They will set their hope on that Son of Man,

> petition Him, and pray for mercy at His hands.

10   Yet the Lord of hosts will press them,

> so they will quickly leave His presence.

Their faces will fill with shame,

> and the darkness deepen on their faces.

11   He will deliver them to the angels for punishment,

---

1 The Messiah; used in the same sense as Dan 7:13-14; Luk 18:31; in total, 81 occurrences in the gospels of the New Testament, all referring to Jesus.

2 Compare Rev 13:8 KJV - *the Lamb slain from the foundation of the world*

3 Compare Rom 8:29; Eph 1:4, 5

4 lit. *sown*

to execute vengeance on them because they have oppressed
His children and His chosen.[1]

12 They will be a spectacle for the righteous and for His chosen,
who will rejoice over them,
because the wrath of the Lord of hosts rests on them,
and His sword is drunk with their blood.

13 The righteous and elect will be saved on that day.
From that time on they will not see the face
of the sinners or the unrighteous.

14 The Lord of hosts will rest over them.
They will eat with the Son of Man,[2] lie down,
and rise up forever and ever.

15 The righteous and chosen will arise from the earth,
and will no longer be depressed.
They will be clothed with garments of glory.

16 These will be the garments of life from the Lord of hosts,[3]
their garments will not grow old,
nor their glory pass away before the Lord of hosts.

Vengeance on the Kings and Mighty

63 IN THOSE days the mighty
and the kings who possess the earth,
will beg for a small delay from His angels of
punishment, to whom they were delivered,
that they might fall down and worship before the
Lord of hosts,
and confess their sins before Him.

2 They will bless and glorify the Lord of hosts,
and say,

---

1 Compare Psa 110:5 - *he will shatter kings on the day of his wrath*
2 Compare Luk 22:16 - *I will not eat it until it is fulfilled in the kingdom of God*
3 Compare Rev 6:11 - *they were each given a white robe*

"Blessed is the Lord of hosts, the Lord of kings,
the Lord of the mighty, the Lord of the rich,
the Lord of glory, and the Lord of wisdom.

3 Your power is splendid in every secret thing
from generation to generation.
Your power lasts from generation to generation,
and Your glory forever and ever.
All your secrets are deep and beyond number,
and your righteousness is beyond comprehension.

4 Now we know that we should glorify and bless the
Lord of kings
and Him who is King over all kings." [1]

5 They will say, "If only we had a reprieve to glorify and give thanks,
and confess our faith in the presence of His glory!

6 Now we long for a little rest, but find none;
we chase after it, but find nothing.
Light has vanished from our presence,
and darkness is our home forever and ever:

7 because we had no faith in Him,
and did not glorify the name of the Lord of hosts,
or show honor to our Lord,
but our hope was in the rulership of our kingdom,
and in our own glory.

8 In the day of our suffering and misery,
He does not save us,
and we have no chance to repent.
Our Lord is true in all His works,
in His judgments, and in His justice.
His judgments show no partiality. [2]

9 We must depart from His presence,

---

1 Compare Rev 19:16 - *King of kings and Lord of lords*
2 Or *his judgments show no respect of persons*; See Rom 2:11 KJV - *For there is no respect of persons with God.* Compare Rom 2:11 - *For God shows no partiality*

because of our *evil* deeds,
and all our sins are rightfully accounted for."

10   Then they will say to themselves,
"Our souls are full of unrighteous gain,
but that won't save us from falling into the flaming
womb of hell."

11   Afterward, their faces will darken with shame
before that Son of Man.
They will be driven from His presence,
and a sword will be ever-before His face when they are near.[1]

12   Then the Lord of hosts said,
"This is the ordinance and judgment against the mighty,
the kings, the exalted, and those who possess the earth
before the Lord of hosts."

The Fallen Angels

64 I SAW other figures
hidden in that place.

2   I heard the voice of the angel saying,
"These are the angels
who descended to the earth,
revealed hidden things
to the children of men,
and seduced the children of men
to commit sin."

Noah Speaks to Enoch

65 IN THOSE days, Noah saw that the earth tilted,
and its destruction was near.

---

1 Compare Rev 19:15 - *From his mouth comes a sharp sword with which to strike
down the nations;* Rev 19:21 - *slain by the sword that came from the mouth of him*

2 He rose from there, went to the ends of the earth,
   and cried aloud to his great-grandfather Enoch.
  Noah said three times with an embittered voice,
   "Hear me, hear me, hear me." [1]

3 And I, *Noah* said to him,
   "Tell me what is happening on the earth
  that the earth is struggling and shaken,
   lest I perish with it."

4 Then there was a powerful disturbance upon the earth,
   a voice spoke from heaven,
   and I fell on my face.

5 Enoch, my great-grandfather, came and stood by me,
   saying to me, "Why have you cried to me
   with a bitter cry and weeping?"

9 [2] Then my great-grandfather Enoch took hold of me by my hand,
   raised me up, and said to me,
  "Go, for I have asked the Lord of hosts about
   this commotion on the earth, and He answered me:
  'Because of their unrighteousness,
   their judgment has been decided,
   and I will not withhold it forever.'

6 A command has gone out from the presence of the Lord
   against those who live on the earth
  that their end is at hand,
   because they know every secret of the angels,
  all the violence of the satans, [3]
   all their powers—the most secret ones—
  all the powers of those who practice sorcery,

---

1 This is not necromancy. Enoch never died, as stated in Heb 11:5 ISV - *Enoch was taken away without experiencing death*
2 Verse order from Charles' notes.
3 *satans*; In the Holy Bible, *satan* is a title for *one who stands opposed*, or *adversary*. It is not used exclusively for the devil. See Strong's Concordance. H7853

the witchcraft of mixing colors,
the powers of those who create molten images for all the earth,

7   how silver is produced from the dust of the earth,
and how soft metal originates in the earth:

8   for lead and tin are not produced from the earth like those are;
it is a fountain that produces them.
An angel stands in it, and that angel is preeminent.

10   Because of the sorceries they have searched out and learned,
the earth and those who live there will be destroyed.

11   And these *fallen angels*—they have no place of repentance forever,
because they showed them what was hidden.
They are the damned."

"But as for you, my son, the Lord of hosts knows that you
are pure and guiltless of this blame concerning the secrets. *1*

12   He has destined your name to be among the holy.
He will preserve you among those who live on the earth,
and has destined your righteous seed for both kingship
and for great honors.
From your descendants will proceed a fountain of the
righteous and holy without number forever."

The Waters Beneath the Earth

66 AFTER THAT, he showed me the angels of punishment *2*
who are ready to open the fountains of water
that are under the earth, *3*
to bring judgment and destruction
over all those who live and dwell on the earth.

2   The Lord of hosts gave a command

---

1 Compare Gen 6:9 - *Noah was a righteous man*
2 Compare Rev 9:15 - *four angels... prepared... to kill a third of mankind*
3 Compare Gen 7:11 - *fountains of the great deep burst forth*

to the angels who went out,

not to raise the great deep

but to watch over it;[1]

for they were the angels over the power of the waters.[2]

3   And I went away from the presence of Enoch.

Noah's Future Descendants

67 IN THOSE days, the voice of God was with me,
and He said to me,

"Noah, your ways[3] have come to my attention,[4]

a life without blame,

a life of love and integrity.[5]

2   Now the angels are making a wooden *structure*,[6]

and when they complete that task

I will place my hand on it and preserve it.

There will come out of it the seed of life,

and a change will set in,

so that the earth will not remain without inhabitants.

3   I will secure your descendants in My presence forever and ever,

and I will spread abroad those who stay with you:[7]

it will not be sterile on the face of the earth,

but they will be blessed and multiply on the earth[8]

in the name of the Lord."

---

1 Compare Rev 7:2-3 - *angels who had been given power to harm earth and sea...*
"Do not harm the earth or the sea... until we have sealed the servants of our God
2 Compare Rev 16:5 - *the angel in charge of the waters*
3 Or *lot;* Or *portion;* Also for both occurrences of *life* in this verse.
4 Or *have come before me*
5 See Gen 6:9 - *Noah was a righteous man, blameless*
6 Enoch 89:1 & Gen 6:14-16, 22 - Noah builds the ark himself. It is unclear if
the angels here are building something that is carried inside the ark, or if it is a
specific piece of the boat itself.
7 Compare Gen 11:8 - *the LORD dispersed them... over the face of all the earth*
8 Compare Gen 9:1 - *multiply and fill the earth*

Angels in the Burning Valley

4   He will imprison those angels of lawlessness, in that burning
        valley
      that my great-grandfather Enoch showed me before,
    in the west among the mountains of gold, silver, iron, soft
        metal, and tin.

5   I saw in that valley a great upheaval
      and a convulsion of the waters.

6   When all this happened,
      caused by that fiery molten metal and the shaking there,
    it produced a smell of sulfur,
      mixed it with the waters;
    and the valley of the angels who led astray *mankind*
      burned beneath the land.

7   Through the valleys of that land run rivers of fire,
      where these angels are punished
      who corrupted those who live on the earth.

8   But the waters of those days will come against[1] the kings,
      the mighty, the exalted, and those who dwell on the earth,
    for the cleansing of the body,
      and the judgment of the spirit.[2]
    Now their spirits are full of lust,
      so they will be punished in their flesh,
      for they have denied the Lord of hosts.
    They perceive their condemnation day by day,
      yet still do not believe in His name.[3]

9   The greater their bodies are burned,

---

1 Or *serve for* (i.e. serve God for the purpose of destroying)
2 Or *the healing of the body, and the punishment of the spirit*
3 Laurence; *see their punishment daily, and yet believe not in His name.*

the greater the correction[1] that takes place in their spirits,
>forever and ever;
for before the Lord of hosts
>none shall speak a careless word.[2]
10   The judgment will come on them
>because they believe in the lust of their flesh
>and deny the Spirit of the Lord.[3]
11   Those same waters will transform in those days;
>for when the angels are punished in those waters,
>the temperature of the springs will change.
When the angels ascend,
>those springs will change and become cold.

Michael's Warning

12   I heard Michael answer, saying,
>"This judgment and its condemnation of the angels
is a warning to the kings and the mighty
>who possess the earth.
13   For these waters of judgment are a cleansing:
>for the body of the kings
>and for the lust of their flesh.
But they will not see and will not believe
>that those waters will change to become a fire
>that burns forever."

---

1 Or *change*
2 Compare Mat 12:36-37 - *on the day of judgment people will give account for every careless word they speak... and by your words you will be condemned.*
3 Compare Mat 12:31-32 - *blasphemy against the Spirit will not be forgiven*

The Book of Enoch Compiled

68 AFTER THAT, my great-grandfather Enoch gave me
the teaching of all the secrets in a book
and the similitudes that were given to him.
He combined them for me, inserted into the book
with the words of the similitudes.

Michael Speaks to Raphael

2   On that day Michael spoke to Raphael, saying,
"The power of the spirit moves me and shakes me
because of the harsh judgment of the secrets,
the judgment over the angels.
Who can endure the harsh judgment that was and is executed,
and before which *the angels* melt away?"

3   Michael spoke again,
saying to Raphael,
"Whose heart is not convicted by this,
and whose self-confidence is not shaken by this word?
Judgment has overtaken them
because of those they led astray."

4   It came to pass when he stood before the Lord of hosts,
Michael said this to Raphael,
"I will not take the *fallen angels'* allotment under the eye of the
Lord;
for the Lord of hosts has been angry with them,
because they act as if they were like the Lord.[1]
5   Therefore all that is hidden will come on them forever and ever;

---

1 Compare Isa 14:10-14 - *I will make myself like the Most High*

for neither angel nor man will hold *the fallen angels' former*
   allotment,
but alone they have received their judgment forever and ever."

Leaders of the Fallen Angels

69
AFTER THIS, they *the fallen angels*, will terrorize and harass
those *that live on the earth*, because this judgment was shown
to those who live on the earth.

2   Behold the names of those angels.
   These are their names:

the first of them is Samyaza, the second Urakaba, the third
Rameel, the fourth Akibeel, the fifth Tamiel, the sixth Ramuel, the
seventh Danel, the eighth Ziquel, the ninth Baraqel, the tenth Azazel,
the eleventh Armaros, the twelfth Matarel, the thirteenth Ananel, the
fourteenth Setawel, the fifteenth Shamshiel, the sixteenth Sahriel, the
seventeenth Ertael, the eighteenth Turel, the nineteenth Tumael, and
the twentieth Yomyael.

The Satans

3   These are the names of the leaders of the *fallen* angels—[1]
   their captains over groups of hundreds, groups of
      fifties, and groups of tens.
4   The name of the first is Yekum:
   that is, the one who led astray all the sons of God,
brought them down to the earth,
   and led them astray through the daughters of men.
5   The second is named Asbeel:
   he gave to the holy sons of God evil advice,

---

1 Or *Satans*

and led them astray to defile their bodies with the daughters
of men.

6   The third is named Gadrel:
who taught the children of men all the martial arts,
and he led astray Eve,[1]
and showed deadly weapons to the sons of men:
the shield, the coat of mail, and the sword for battle.
He revealed all the instruments of death to the children of men.[2]

7   From his hand, they overpowered those living on the earth
from that day and forever more.

8   The fourth was named Penemue:
he taught the children of men both the bitter and the sweet;
he taught them all the secrets of their wisdom.

9   He instructed mankind in writing with ink and paper,
and many have used that to sin from age to age and until
this day.[3]

10   For men were not born for this,[4]
there should be no need to confirm their faith
with pen and ink.

11   For man was not created differently from the angels
in the sense that they should remain just and pure.[5]
Death, which destroys everything, would not have touched them,
but through their knowledge they are perishing,[6]
and death then consumes us through this power.[7]

---

1 Compare Gen 3:13 ISV - *"The Shining One misled me," the woman answered*
2 These teachings are also ascribed to Azazel in Enoch 8:1
3 Compare Pro 10:19; Ecc 10:14 - *When words are many, transgression is not lacking;* Note that the writer does not condemn writing itself, but how many have used it.
4 Compare Gen 2:25 - *man and his wife were both naked and were not ashamed*
5 Compare Gen 1:31 - *God saw everything that he had made... it was very good*
6 Compare Gen 2:17 - *knowledge of good and evil... you shall surely die*
7 Compare Gen 3:22 - *the LORD God said, "Behold, the man has become like one of us in knowing good and evil. Now, lest he reach out his hand and take also of the tree of life and eat, and live forever—"*

12   The fifth was named Kasyade:

>   He taught the children of men all the wicked attacks of spirits
>   and demons.
>
> taught abortion of the embryo in the womb, that it should die,
>   and taught striking the spirit through serpent bites.
>
> *He taught* the attack delivered at midday [1]
>   by the offspring of the serpent, whose name is Tabaet.

The Oath

13   This is the task of Kesbel,

>   the chief of the oath which he revealed to the holy ones
> while he stayed high above in glory,
>   and its name is Beka.

14   He asked Michael to show him the hidden name, [2]

>   that he might pronounce it in the oath,
> so those who revealed the secrets to the children of men
>   would be afraid because of that name and oath.

15   This is the power of the oath, for it is powerful and strong,

>   and he placed this oath Akae in the hand of Michael.

16   And these are the secrets of this oath . . . [3]

> They are strong through His oath: [4]
>   the heavens were suspended
> before the world was created and forever. [5]

---

1 Compare Psa 91:5-6 LXX - *the evil spirit at noon-day.*
2 Compare Rev 19:12 ISV - *He (Jesus) has a name written on him that nobody
knows except himself;* Heb 1:3-5 - *the word of his power... a more excellent name*
3 Missing passage
4 This oath seems connected to Jesus (that Son of Man) and his name. See
verses 14, 16, 18, 26, 29 and their footnotes.
5 Compare Col 1:16 - *For by him* (Jesus) *all things in heaven and on earth were
created... All things have been created through him and for him.*

17 Through it the earth was founded upon the water.[1]

From the secret recesses of the mountains come beautiful
waters,

from the creation of the world and unto eternity.

18 Through that oath the sea was created,[2]

and to limit it, He set for it the sand

against the time of *its* anger.

It dare not pass beyond it

from the creation of the world unto eternity.[3]

19 Through that oath the depths are made secure,[4]

endure, and do not move from their place

from eternity to eternity.

20 Through that oath the sun and moon complete their course,

and do not violate their orders

from eternity to eternity.

21 Through that oath the stars complete their route;

He calls them by their names,[5]

and they answer Him from eternity to eternity.

22 So do the spirits of the water, of the winds, and of all breezes,

their paths *coming* from all the quarters of the winds.

23 Preserved inside it are the voices of the thunder

and the light of the lightning.

The chambers of the hail are preserved there

and the chambers of the frost,

the chambers of the mist,

---

1 Compare Psa 24:1-2 - *The earth is the LORD's... he has founded it upon the seas;*
Psa 136:6 ISV - *the one who spread out the earth over the waters*
2 Compare Joh 1:3 ISV - *Through him (Jesus) all things were made, and apart
from him nothing was made that has been made.*
3 Compare Jer 5:22 - *I placed the sand as the boundary for the sea, a perpetual
barrier that it cannot pass*
4 Compare Pro 8:28 - *he established the fountains of the deep*
5 Compare Psa 147:4 - *stars; he gives to all of them their names*

the chambers of the rain and the dew.[1]

24   All these believe and give thanks before the Lord of hosts,
        and glorify *Him* with all their power.
      Their sustenance is in every act of thanksgiving:
        they thank, glorify, and praise
        the name of the Lord of hosts forever and ever.

25   This oath is mighty over them,
        through it they are preserved,
      their paths are preserved,
        and their course is not destroyed.
26   There was great joy among them,
        and they blessed, glorified, and praised,
        because the name of that Son of Man was revealed to them.[2]
27   He sat on the throne of His glory,
        and all judgment was given to the Son of Man.[3]
      He caused the sinners to vanish[4]
        and be destroyed from off the face of the earth.[5]

---

1 According to Gen 2:5-6 it might not have rained prior to the time of the
great flood. However, it can be assumed that the storehouses of the rain were
already prepared for their future use. Compare Job 38:22, 24 - *the storehouses of
the snow... storehouses of the hail... the place where the light is distributed, or where
the east wind is scattered upon the earth*
2 Compare Rev 14:1 - *who had his* (Jesus') *name and his Father's name written on
their foreheads*
3 Compare Joh 5:22 - *The Father judges no one, but has given all judgment to the
Son*
4 Compare Mat 13:38-39, 30 - *The weeds are the sons of the evil one; The harvest
is the end of the age, and the reapers are angels; Gather the weeds first and bind
them in bundles to be burned;* Luk 17:30, 34, 37 - *so will it be on the day when the
Son of Man is revealed; One will be taken and the other left; "Where, Lord?" He said
to them, "Where the corpse is, there the vultures will gather."*
5 Compare Rev 19:11, 21 - *Then I saw heaven opened, and behold, a white horse!
The one sitting on it is called Faithful and True, and in righteousness he judges and
makes war; The rest were killed by the sword that belonged to* (Jesus)

Those who have led the world astray,
28   they will be bound with chains.
They will be assembled for destruction,
    imprisoned there,
and all their works will vanish
    from the face of the earth.
29   From then on there will be nothing corruptible;
For that Son of Man has appeared,
    and has seated Himself on the throne of His glory.
All evil shall pass away before His face.
The word of that Son of Man will go out
    and be strong before the Lord of hosts.

This is the third similitude of Enoch.

God Takes Enoch

70 IT LATER happened
that *Enoch's* name lifted up
during the years of his life
    and raised up before that Son of Man
and before the Lord of hosts,[1]
    away from those who live on the earth.
2   He raised up on the chariots of the wind,[2]
    and his name vanished among them.

3   From that day I was no longer numbered among them.[3]
    He set me between the two winds, between the North
        and the West,

---

1 Compare Heb 11:5 ISV - *Enoch... before he was taken, he won approval as one who pleased God*
2 Compare 2Ki 2:11 - *chariots of fire... Elijah went up by a whirlwind into heaven*
3 Compare Gen 5:24 - *Enoch walked with God, and he was not, for God took him.*

where the angels took the cords to measure for me the place
>for the elect and righteous.

4   There I saw the first fathers and the righteous
>who have dwelled there since the beginning.

A Previous Vision of Enoch

71
1   ANOTHER TIME, this came to pass:
my spirit was hidden away,[1]
it ascended into the heavens,
>and I saw the holy sons of God.
They were stepping on flames of fire:[2]
>their robes were white, as were their tunics,
>and their faces were bright like snow.

2   I saw two streams of fire,[3]
>and the light of that fire shone like hyacinth.
I fell on my face before the Lord of hosts.

3   The angel Michael, one of the archangels,[4] seized me by my
>right hand, lifted me up
>and led me out to *the places of* all the secret *things.*[5]
He showed me all the hidden truths of mercy
>and of righteousness.

4   He showed me all secrets of the farthest heavens,
>all the repositories of the stars,
all the heavenly lights,
>and how they travel before the holy ones.

---

1 Compare 2Co 12:2 - *caught up to the third heaven—whether in the body or out of the body I do not know*
2 Compare Eze 28:14 ISV - *cherub... you walked in the midst of fiery stones*
3 Compare Dan 7:10 - *A river of fire flowed out from before him*
4 Compare Jude 1:9 - *the archangel Michael*; 1Th 4:16 - *the voice of an archangel*
5 Compare Dan 10:21 - *I will tell you what is inscribed in the book of truth*

A Second Vision of Enoch

5   The Spirit translated[1] me into the heaven of heavens,[2]
          and I saw there as it were a structure built of crystals,
          and between those crystals, tongues of living fire.

6   My spirit saw the ring that encircled that house of fire,
          and on its four sides were streams full of living fire
          that encircled the house.

7   Round about were seraphim, cherubim, and ophanim:[3]
          these are those who never sleep
          and guard the throne of His glory.

8   I saw angels beyond number,
          a thousand thousands, and ten thousand times ten thousand,
          encircling that habitation.
       Michael, Raphael, Gabriel, and Phanuel,
          and the holy angels who are above the heavens,
          enter and leave that habitation.

9   They came out of that habitation:
          Michael, Gabriel, Raphael, and Phanuel,
          and many holy angels without number.

10   With them was the Ancient of Days,[4]
          His head white and pure as wool,
          and His raiment indescribable.

11   I fell on my face;
          my whole body grew faint;
          and my spirit was humbled.[5]
       I cried with a loud voice,

---

1 Compare Eze 37:1 ISV - *brought me out by the Spirit of the LORD to... a valley*
2 Compare Eze 8:3 ISV - *the Spirit lifted me up between the earth and sky*
3 Hebrew word for *wheel* used in Eze 1:15-21; Eze 10:2, 6, 9-13; See Dan 7:9
4 Or *Head of Days;* so in verse 14.
5 Or *was changed*

. . .with the spirit of power, *1*

    and blessed, glorified, and exalted.

12   These blessings that came from my mouth

    became acceptable before that Ancient of Days.

13   The Ancient of Days came with Michael, Gabriel,

        Raphael, and Phanuel,

    and thousands and ten thousands of angels without number.

[Another was with Him whose face had the appearance of a man,

    and His face was full of grace like one of the holy angels.

I asked the angel who went with me and showed me all

        the hidden things,

    about that Son of Man, who He was, where He was from,

    and why He went with the Ancient of Days?] *2*

14   The angel came to me, greeted me with his voice,

    and said to me,

"This is the Son of Man *3* who is born unto righteousness;

    righteousness remains on Him, *4*

and the righteousness of the Ancient of Days never leaves Him."

15   *And the angel* said to me, "He proclaims to you peace

    in the name of the world to come; *5*

for this has been a reason for peace

    since the creation of the world,

and so will it be to you forever

    and from eternity to eternity.

---

1 Beginning of line missing in manuscript

2 This is a lost passage reconstructed from Enoch 46:1-2. Because of the missing passage, an ancient scribe altered verses 14 and 16, trying to describe the Son of Man as being Enoch. Charles notes that this is a clear alteration of the manuscripts. Enoch 46 and other chapters make it abundantly clear that the books of Enoch do not interpret Enoch himself to be the Son of Man.

3 The Messiah; used in the same sense as Dan 7:13-14; Luk 18:31; in total, 81 occurrences in the gospels of the New Testament, all referring to Jesus.

4 Compare Isa 11:5 - *Righteousness shall be the belt of his waist, and faithfulness the belt of his loins.*

5 *to come*; Compare Eph 1:21 - *not only in this age but also in the one to come*

16   All will walk in His ways because righteousness never leaves Him:
       they will live with Him, and with Him is their inheritance,
       and they will not be separated from Him forever and ever and ever.

17   So there will be eternal life[1] with the Son of Man,
       and the righteous will have peace and a straight path
       in the name of the Lord of hosts forever and ever."

---

1 Or *length of days*

5 ENOCH

Luminaries

An Angel Teaches About the Heavens

72 THIS IS the book of the paths of the heavenly lights:
how they relate to each other according to their types,
their dominion, and their seasons,
according to their names,[1] where they rise,
and according to their months.
The conductor[2] *of the luminaries* is Uriel, the holy angel who
accompanied me and explained these things.
He showed me all their laws exactly as they are,[3]
and how *these laws*[4] will last for all the *remaining* years of the
world forever,[5]
until the new creation is accomplished that endures eternal.[6]

The Sun

2   This is the first law of the heavenly lights:

---

1 Compare Psa 147:4 - *stars; he gives to all of them their names*
2 Or *guide*
3 Compare Jer 31:35 ISV - *the laws that govern the moon and stars*
4 Compare Job 38:33 - *Do you know the laws of the heavens?*
5 Compare Psa 148:3-6 - *sun and moon... shining stars... he established them
forever and ever*
6 Compare Isa 65:17; 66:22 - *"For behold, I create new heavens and a new earth,
and the former things shall not be remembered or come into mind.*

the great light, the sun, rises in the eastern passageways[1] of
the heavens,
and sets in the western passageways of the heavens.[2]

3 I saw six passageways through which the sun emerges,[3]
and six passageways through which the sun sets.[4]
The moon rises and sets in these passageways,
and the first of the stars and those they come before:[5]
six in the east and six in the west,
all following properly each after the other
passing many windows to the south and north of these
passageways.

4 First rises the great light named the sun,[6]
and his roundness is like the circumference of the heavens.
He is complete with illumination and flaming fire.

5 The chariot he rises on is driven by the wind,
and the sun sets in the sky and returns through
the north to reach the east.
He is led to reach that passageway
and shines in the sky.

6 So he rises in the first month[7] in the great passageway,
which is the fourth of those six passageways in the east.

7 Inside that fourth passageway—through which the sun rises in
the first month—are twelve open windows,
and a flame comes out of them when they are opened
in their season.

8 When the sun rises in the heavens,

---

1 Or *signs of the zodiac*; so throughout chapter 72. See Job 9:9 - *chambers*
2 Compare Psa 19:4 ISV - *He has set up a tent for the sun in the heavens*
3 Capricornus, Aquarius, Pisces, Aries, Taurus, and Gemini
4 Cancer, Leo, Virgo, Libra, Scorpio, and Sagittarius.
5 Compare Isa 40:26 - *He who brings out their host by number*
6 Compare Gen 1:16 - *two great lights—the greater light to rule the day*
7 April; Exo 13:4 ISV - *the month of Abib;* the ecclesiastical year; Neh 2:1 ISV - *the month of Nissan;* Abib was called Nissan after the exile.

he comes out through that fourth passageway thirty mornings
in succession,
and sets accurately *¹* in the fourth passageway in the west
of the heavens.

9   During this period the day becomes daily longer
and the night, nightly shorter to the thirtieth morning.

10 On that day, the day is longer than the night by a ninth part.
The day amounts exactly to ten parts
and the night to eight parts.

11 The sun rises from that fourth passageway
and sets in the fourth.
He returns to the fifth passageway of the east for thirty mornings,
and rises from it and sets in the fifth passageway.

12 Then the day becomes longer by one part and amounts to
eleven parts,
and the night becomes shorter and amounts to seven parts.

13 He returns to the east and enters the sixth passageway,
and rises and sets in the sixth passageway
thirty-one mornings on account of its sign. *²*

14 On that day, the day becomes longer than the night,
and the day becomes double the night.
The day becomes twelve parts,
and the night is shortened and becomes six parts.

15 The sun rises up to make the day shorter and the night longer.
The sun returns to the east and enters the sixth passageway,
rises from it and sets thirty mornings.

16 When thirty mornings are complete, the day shortens by exactly
one part,
and becomes eleven parts, and the night seven.

17 The sun goes out from that sixth passageway in the west,

---

1 Compare Psa 104:19 - *the sun knows its time for setting*
2 *its sign* - the summer solstice

goes to the east, and rises in the fifth passageway for thirty
    mornings,
and sets in the west again in the fifth western passageway.[1]

18   On that day, the day shortens by one part,
and amounts to ten parts and the night to eight parts.

19   The sun emerges from that fifth passageway and sets in the fifth
    passageway of the west,
and rises in the fourth passageway for thirty-one mornings
    because of its sign,[2]
and sets in the west.

20   On that day, the day is equalized with the night, and becomes
    of equal length,
and the night amounts to nine parts and the day to nine parts.

21   The sun rises from that passageway, sets in the west,
returns to the east and rises thirty mornings in the third
    passageway,
and sets in the west in the third passageway.

22   On that day, the night becomes longer than the day,
night becomes longer than night,
and day shorter than day until the thirtieth morning.
Then the night amounts to exactly ten parts, and the day to
    eight parts.

23   The sun rises from that third passageway
sets in the third passageway in the west, returns to the east,
and for thirty mornings rises in the second passageway
    in the east,
and in the same way sets in the second passageway in the west
    of the heavens.

24   On that day, the night amounts to eleven parts
and the day to seven parts.

---

1 Compare Job 9:9 - *who made the Bear and Orion, the Pleiades and the chambers of the south*
2 *its sign* - the winter solstice

25 The sun rises on that day from that second passageway and sets
      in the west in the second passageway,
   returns to the east into the first passageway for thirty-one
      mornings,
   and sets in the first passageway in the west of the heavens.

26 On that day, the night becomes longer and amounts to
      double of the day:
   and the night amounts to exactly twelve parts, and the day
      to six.

27 So the sun has traveled every section of his orbit,
   goes back again to travel those sections,
enters that passageway thirty mornings,
   and sets in the west opposite to it.

28 On that night, the night grows shorter than the day by
      a ninth part,
   and the night has become eleven parts and the day seven parts.

29 The sun has returned and entered into the second passageway
      in the east,
   and returns to his ordered course for thirty mornings, rising
      and setting.

30 On that day, the night becomes shorter,
   the night amounts to ten parts and the day to eight.

31 On that day, the sun rises from that passageway and sets
      in the west,
   returns to the east, rises in the third portal for thirty-one
      mornings,
   and sets in the west of the heavens.

32 On that day, the night decreases and amounts to nine parts,
   the day to nine parts, and the night is equal to the day,

and the days of the year are figured 364.[1]

33   The length of the daytime and of the nighttime,

        and the shortness of the daytime and of the nighttime—

        these fluctuate according to the course of the sun.

34   Therefore, his course becomes longer daily,

        and his course shorter nightly.

35   This is the law and the course of the sun,

        and of his return each day:

sixty times he returns and rises.

        This is the great light, called the sun, forever and ever.[2]

36   Therefore, the one that rises is the great light,

        and he is named based on his appearance,

        just as the Lord commanded.

37   As he rises, so he sets

        and does not diminish, and does not rest,

        but runs day and night.[3]

His light is seven times brighter

        than *the light* of the moon;[4]

        but in *relative* size they are both equal.

The Moon and its Phases

73 AFTER THIS law, I beheld another law
dealing with the smaller light named the moon.[5]

2   Her roundness is like the circumference of the heavens,

        the chariot she rides is driven by the wind,

---

1 Or *365*; Charles notes, "Enoch was early regarded as the teacher of the solar year of 365 days, owing to the significant duration of his life."; Gen 5:23 ISV - *Enoch lived a total of 365 years*

2 Compare Psa 72:5; 17 - *the sun endures… throughout all generations*

3 Compare Ecc 1:5 - *The sun rises, and the sun goes down, and hastens to the place where it rises*

4 Compare Isa 30:26 ISV - *the moon… the sun's light will be seven times brighter*

5 Compare Gen 1:16 ISV - *two great lights… the smaller light to shine during the night*

and light is given to her in measured amounts.

3   Her rising and setting change every month:[1]
    her days are like the days of the sun,
and when her light is full it equals one seventh of the light of
      the sun.

4   Thus she rises:
her first phase in the east comes out on the thirtieth morning.
On that day she becomes visible
    and forms the first phase of the moon
on the thirtieth day together with the sun
    in the passageway where the sun rises.

5   Each half of her has seven parts,
    and her whole orb[2] is empty, without light;
except for one-seventh part of it:
    the fourteenth part of her light.

6   When she receives one-seventh part of the half of her light,
    her light amounts to one-seventh part and the half of it.

7   She sets with the sun,
    and when the sun rises the moon rises with him,
receives half of one part of light,
    and in that night, in the beginning of her morning,
at the start of the lunar day, the moon sets with the sun,
    and is invisible that night with the fourteen parts and the
      half of one of them.

8   She rises on that day with exactly a seventh part,
    comes out, recedes from the rising of the sun,
and in her remaining days she becomes bright
    in the *remaining* thirteen parts.

---

1 Compare Psa 104:19 ISV - *He made the moon to mark time*
2 Or *circle*

The Lunar Year

74

1 I SAW another course: a law for *the moon,*
how according to that law she performs her
monthly revolution.

2 Uriel, the holy angel who is the conductor[1] of them all,
showed all these *phases of the moon* and their positions to me.
I wrote down their positions as he showed them to me;
I wrote down their months as they were,
and the appearance of their lights until fifteen days
were completed.

3 *In one half,* each of her seven portions
complete all her light in the east,
In the other half, each of her seven portions
complete all her darkness in the west.

4 In certain months, she alters her settings,
and in certain months, she pursues her own peculiar course.

5 During two months, the moon sets with the sun
in those two middle passageways[2]—*meaning* the third and
fourth passageways.

6 She comes out seven days,
turns about and returns again by the passageway where
the sun rises.
In that *course* she completes all her light and recedes from the sun.
For eight days *she* enters the sixth passageway through which
the sun comes out.

7 When the sun comes out of the fourth passageway, she goes
out seven days,
until she goes out from the fifth
and turns back again in seven days into the fourth passageway
and accomplishes all her light.

---

1 Or *guide*
2 Or *signs of the zodiac*; see notes on Enoch 72:2-3; so throughout Chapter 74

And she recedes, entering the first passageway in eight days.

8   She returns again in seven days into the fourth passageway
      where the sun emerges.

9   Thus I saw their position—how the moon rose and the sun
        set in those days.

10 If five years are added together
      the sun has a surplus of thirty days.
    All the days totaled for one of those five years,
      when they are full, amount to 364 days.[1]

11 The surplus of the sun and of the stars totals six days:
        in five years—six days every year—come to thirty days:
    and the moon falls behind the sun and stars by thirty days.

12 The sun and the stars bring in all the years with precision.
      They do not advance or delay their positions by a single
            day unto eternity,
      but complete the years as they should in 364 days.

13 In three years there are 1,092 days,
      and in five years 1,820 days,
      thus in 8 years there are 2,912 days.

14 For the moon alone—the number of days in three years is 1,062,
      and in five years she falls 50 days behind.[2]

15 In five years there are 1,770 days,
      thus in eight years the moon has 2,832 days.

16 For in eight years she falls behind by eighty days.

17 The year completes, matching precisely with their fixed
            positions in the heavens
      and with the positions of the sun—rising from the
            passageways where it rises and sets for thirty days.

---

1 Or *365*; Charles notes, "Enoch was early regarded as the teacher of the solar year of 365 days, owing to the significant duration of his life."; Gen 5:23 ISV - *Enoch lived a total of 365 years*; so also in verse 12
2 i.e. to the sum of 1,770 add 1,000 and 62 days.

The Luminaries and Their Leaders

75 THE LEADERS over the chiefs of the thousands, who are
placed over the whole creation and over all the stars,[1]
are also *leaders over* the four inserted days,
which cannot be separated from their places,[2] according to
the calculation of the year,
and these serve during the four days that are not
calculated in the total of the year.

2   Men make errors about them *when adding up the year*,
for those heavenly lights work at the right place and time
based on their fixed positions in the heavens:
one *day* in the first passageway,[3] one in the third passageway
of the heavens,
one in the fourth passageway, and one in the sixth passageway,
and the exactness of the year is completed by 364
separate stations.

3   For the signs,[4] the times, the years, and the days
the angel Uriel showed to me,
whom the Lord of glory has set over all the heavenly lights
of the heavens forever,[5]
in both the heavens and in the world,
that *the lights* should rule[6] on the face of the heavens
and be seen on the earth,
and be leaders for the daytime and the night:
the sun, moon, and stars,

---

1 Compare 1Co 15:41 WEB - *one star differs from another star in glory*
2 Compare Jer 31:35 - *the fixed order of the moon and the stars*
3 Or *sign of the zodiac*; see notes on Enoch 72:2-3; so throughout Chapter 75
4 Of the zodiac
5 Compare Psa 89:36-37 - *as long as the sun before me. Like the moon it shall be established forever*
6 Compare Psa 136:8-9 - *the sun to rule over the day... the moon and stars to rule over the night*

and all the created things that serve,[1]
 each making its orbit in the heavenly chariots.

Heat of the Sun

4 In the same way, Uriel showed me twelve openings on the
     sun's circular chariot in the heavens
   through which the rays of the sun shine out.
  From these *openings* warmth is spread over the earth,[2]
   when they are opened at their appointed seasons.

5   ...[3]

More Openings

6 As for the twelve passageways in the heavens, at the ends of
     the earth,
   out of which emerge the sun, moon, and stars,[4]
   and all the works of heaven in the east and in the west;

7 there are many openings to the north and south of them:
   each opening in its time to produce warmth.
  So, there are also passageways where the stars emerge
   as they are commanded,
   and where they set according to their number.

8 I saw chariots in the heavens, moving through outer space
   above those passageways where the stars that never set turn.[5]

9 One *passageway* is larger than all the rest,
   and it makes its course across the entire world.

---

1 *that serve*; Compare Psa 148:3; Deu 4:19; Job 31:26-28
2 Compare Psa 19:6 - *there is nothing hidden from its heat*
3 Verse 5 was composed of manuscript errors that did not form an actual
verse. Charles notes, "The entire verse is... to be rejected as an intrusion."
4 Compare Psa 19:6 - *Its rising is from the end of the heavens, and its circuit to the
end of them*
5 Or *resolve*

The Twelve Winds and Their Portals

76

AT THE ends of the earth, I saw twelve portals open for all the winds,

    where the winds emerge and blow over the earth.[1]

2   Three of them are open on the face of the heavens,[2]

      three in the west, three on the south of the heavens,

      and three on the north.

3   The first three are to the east, and three are to the north,

      and after those to the north:

      three to the south, and three to the west.

4   Through four of them blow winds of blessing and prosperity.

    From the *remaining* eight blow hurtful winds:

      when they are sent, they bring destruction

  on all the earth, on the water upon it,

      on all who live on *the earth*,

  and on everything that is in the water

      and on the land.

5   The first wind from those portals, called the east wind,

      emerges from the first portal in the east, nearest the south:

      from it comes desolation, drought, heat, and destruction.

6   Through the second portal in the middle comes what is fitting:

      from it comes rain, fruitfulness, prosperity, and dew.

    Out of the third portal, nearest to the north,

      comes cold and drought.

7   After these the south winds come out of three portals.

    Through the first portal, nearest the east,

      comes a hot wind.

8   Through the middle portal next to it

---

1 Compare Psa 135:7 - *the end of the earth... wind from his storehouses*

2 the east

comes fragrant smells, dew, rain, prosperity, and health.

9   Through the third portal nearest the west
       comes dew, rain, blight, and desolation.

10   After these *come* the north winds.
      From the seventh portal in the east
        comes dew, rain, locusts, and desolation.

11   From the middle portal comes what is fitting:
        health, rain, dew, and prosperity.
      Through the third portal in the west
        comes cloud, frost, snow, rain, dew, and blight.

12   After these, the fourth *quarter* is the west winds.
      Through the first portal nearest the north
        comes dew, hail, cold, snow, and frost.

13   From the middle portal
        comes dew, rain, prosperity, and blessing.
      Through the last portal nearest the south
        comes drought, desolation, burning, and destruction.

14   The twelve portals of the four quarters of the heavens
        are thus completed.
      All their laws, all their plagues, and all their benefits
        I have shown to you, my son Methuselah.

The Four Quarters of the World

77 THE FIRST quarter is called the east,
      because it is the first;
and the second, the south,
      because the Most High will descend there.

Indeed, in that place
> He who is blessed forever will descend.

2 The west quarter is named the diminished
> because that is where all the lights in the heavens
> fade and set.

3 The fourth quarter, named the north,
> is divided into three parts.

The first of them
> is for the dwelling of men.

The second contains seas of water,
> the abysses, forests, rivers, darkness, and clouds.

The third part
> contains the garden of righteousness.

Seven Mountains and Seven Rivers

4 I saw seven high mountains,
> higher than all the mountains on the earth.

Frost emerges from there,
> and *from there* days, seasons, and years pass by.[1]

5 I saw seven rivers on the earth larger than all the rivers:
> one of them coming from the desert
> pours its waters into the Great Sea.[2]

6 The *next* two[3] come from the north to the sea
> and pour their waters into the Erythraean Sea[4] in the east.

7 The remaining four[5]
> come out on the side of the north to their own sea,
> two of them to the Erythraean Sea, and two into the Great Sea

---

1 Compare Gen 1:14 ISV - *lights... to act as signs for seasons, days, and years*
2 Compare Num 34:6-7 - *the Great Sea;* the Mediterranean
3 *next two* - The Euphrates and Tigris rivers
4 *Erythraean Sea* - A general name for the Arabian, Persian, and Indian seas.
5 *remaining four* - the Indus, Ganges, Oxus, and Jaxartes rivers

and discharge themselves there,
and some say, "Into the desert."

8   Seven great islands I saw in the sea and in the mainland:
two in the mainland and five in the Great Sea.

The Sun and Moon

78
THE NAMES of the sun are the following:
the first Aryares and the second Tomas.[1]

2   The moon has four names:
the first name is Asonya, the second Ebla, the third Benase,
and the fourth Erae.[2]

3   These are the two great lights:[3]
their roundness is like the roundness of the heavens,
and the *relative* size of both circumferences is the same.

4   Within the circumference of the sun, the light is seven times
brighter than the light of the moon.[4]

That light is gradually transferred until *the moon is full*,
reaching a full seventh of the sun's brightness.

5   They set and enter the passageways[5] of the west,
and make their revolutions by the north,
and rise through the eastern passageways
on the face of the heavens.

6   When the moon rises, she appears in the heavens
with one-fourteenth of her light.

After fourteen more days, her light becomes full.

7   Also fifteen parts of light are added to her,
so that on the fifteenth day her light is full,

---

1 These names correspond to the two seasons of the year in Israel; Aryares
when the sun is cool in the winter, and Tomas in the heat of summer.
2 Possibly connected to the phases of the moon.
3 Compare Psa 136:7 - *the great lights*
4 Compare Isa 30:26 ISV - *the moon... the sun's light will be seven times brighter*
5 Or *constellations* or *signs of the zodiac*; so throughout chapter 78

according to the sign of the year.

She becomes fifteen parts,

and the moon grows by *the addition of* fourteenth parts.

8   In her waning, *the moon* decreases on the first day to fourteen
          parts of her light,

on the second to thirteen parts of light, on the third to twelve,

on the fourth to eleven, on the fifth to ten, on the sixth to nine,

on the seventh to eight, on the eighth to seven,

on the ninth to six, on the tenth to five, on the eleventh to four,

on the twelfth to three, on the thirteenth to two,

on the fourteenth to the half of a seventh,

and all her remaining light disappears wholly on the fifteenth.

9   In certain months, the month has twenty-nine days

and once twenty-eight.

10   Uriel showed me another law:

when light is transferred to the moon,

and on which side it is transferred to her by the sun.

11   During the whole time when the moon is growing in her light,

she transfers *the light* to herself when opposite to the sun.

Within fourteen days her light is accomplished in the heavens;

when she is completely lit,

her light is *then* accomplished full in the heavens.

12   On the first day, she is called the new moon,

for on that day the light rises upon her.

13   She becomes the full moon exactly on the day

when the sun sets in the west.

From the east she rises at night,

and the moon shines the whole night through

until the sun rises opposite *from* her,

and the moon is seen opposite the sun.

14   On the side where the moonlight shines,

there again she wanes until all the light vanishes,

all the days of the month are at an end,

> her circumference is empty,

> and *she is* void of light.

15 She makes three months of thirty days each,

> and other times she makes three months of twenty-nine

> > days each,

where she finishes waning in the first period of time,

> and in the first passageway for one hundred and

> > seventy-seven days.

16 In the time of her going out,[1] she appears for three months of

> > thirty days each,

> and she appears for three months of twenty-nine days each.

17 At night, the moon appears like *the face of* a man for twenty days

> > at a time,

> and by day looks like the sky,

for there is nothing *to see of* her except her light.

Review of Laws

7 9 NOW, MY son, I have shown you everything,

> and the law of all the stars of the heavens is completed.

2 *The angel Uriel* showed me all their laws for every day,

> for every time, for every jurisdiction, and for every year.

He showed me the moon's departure,

> according to her order in each month and in every week;

3 and the waning of the moon

> that happens in the sixth passageway.

For in this sixth passageway, her light is full,

> and after that the waning begins.

4 *That waning* happens in the first passageway in its season,

> until one hundred and seventy-seven days have passed:

---

1 i. e. in the second half of the year

calculated in weeks as twenty-five *weeks* and two days.

5   She falls behind the sun and the order of the stars exactly five
              days in the course of one period,*1*
       after traveling this place that you see.

6   Such is the appearance and likeness of every heavenly light
              that Uriel the archangel, who is their conductor,*2* showed me.

The Earth Will Go Astray

80 IN THOSE days, the angel Uriel answered,
              saying to me,
       "Behold, I have shown you everything, Enoch.
              I have revealed everything so you would see
       the sun, the moon, the leaders of the stars of the heavens,
              and all those who turn them: their tasks, times, and
                     departures."

2   "In the days of the sinners,
              the spring rain will be shortened.
       Their crops will come late
              in their lands and fields.
       All things on the earth will alter,
              and will not appear in their time.
       The rain will be kept back,*3*
              and the heavens will refrain.*4*

3   In those times, the fruits of the earth will be delayed,
              and will not grow in season.
       The fruits of the trees will be withheld in their time."

------

1 half a year
2 Or *guide*
3 Compare Jer 3:3 - *spring rain has not come; yet... you refuse to be ashamed*
4 Compare Jer 5:24-25 - *rain in its season... Your iniquities have turned these away*

4   "The moon will alter her order,
        and not appear at her time.[1]

5   In those days, the sun will rise in the evening,[2]
        and his great chariot will journey to the west,
    causing distress [3] *as it goes*,
        and will shine much brighter than its usual light.

6   Many chiefs of the stars will violate their orders.[4]
    They will alter their orbits and tasks,
        and not appear in their usual seasons.

7   The whole order of the stars
        will be concealed from the sinners.
    The thoughts of those on the earth will go astray,
        and they will turn aside from all their ways.
    Indeed, they will falsely believe *the hosts of heaven* are gods.[5]

8   Evil will multiply over them,
        and punishment will come on them
        to destroy all."

The Mission of Enoch

81

1   HE SAID to me,
    "Observe, Enoch, these heavenly tablets,
    read what is written on them,
        and mark every individual fact."

2   I observed the heavenly tablets,
        read everything that was written,

---

1 Compare Jos 10:12-13 - *And the sun stood still, and the moon stopped*
2 Compare Amo 8:9 - *I will make the sun go down at noon and darken the earth in broad daylight*
3 Compare Luk 21:25 - *there will be signs in sun and moon and stars, and on the earth distress of nations*
4 Compare Rev 6:13 - *the stars of the sky fell*
5 Compare Act 7:42 - *But God turned away and gave them over to worship the host of heaven*

and understood everything.

I read the book containing all the deeds of mankind,
and *read about* all the children of flesh that will be on the earth
to the farthest generations.

3   At once I blessed the great Lord, the King of glory forever,
because He made all the works of the world.

I praised the Lord because of His patience,
and blessed Him because of the children of men.

4   After that I said,

"Blessed is the man who dies in righteousness and goodness:
no record of wickedness is written about Him,[1]
and there is no day of judgment against Him."

Enoch Returns Home

5   Those seven holy ones carried me and placed me on the
earth before the door of my house,

saying to me, "Declare everything to your son, Methuselah;
show all your children that no flesh is righteous[2] in the
sight of the Lord, for He created them.

6   For one year, we will leave you with your son,
until you give your commands,

that you may teach your children, write for them,
and testify to all your children.

In the second year, *the angels* will take you *away* from among them.

7   Let your heart be strong,
for the godly will announce righteousness to the godly;

the righteous will rejoice with *those who are* righteous,
and will offer congratulation to one another.

8   But the sinners will die with the sinners,

---

1 Compare Isa 45:25 - *I, (the Lord) I am he who blots out your transgressions for
my own sake, and I will not remember your sins.*
2 Compare Job 9:2 - *how can a man be in the right before God?*

and the backsliders go will down with the backsliders.

9 Those who practice righteousness will die
    because of the deeds of men,
    and are taken away because of the evil of the godless." [1]

10 In those days, *the angels* stopped speaking to me,
    and I came to my people, blessing the Lord of the whole earth. [2]

Preserve the Books of Enoch

82 NOW, MY son Methuselah, all these things I am telling you and writing down for you.
I have taught you everything,
    and given you books about these things.
So preserve, my son Methuselah, the books from your
        father's hand,
    and deliver them to the generations of the world.

2 I have given wisdom to you, your children,
    and your descendants, [3]
for them to pass to their children for generations
    this surpassing wisdom.

3 Those who understand it will fight off sleep
    to hear and learn this wisdom.
For those that eat of it,
    it will please them better than good food. [4]

A Righteous Year

4 Blessed are all the righteous.

---

1 Compare Isa 57:1 - *the righteous man is taken away from calamity*; 2Ki 22:20 - *I will gather you to your fathers, and you shall be gathered to your grave in peace*
2 Compare Psa 89:11 - *the earth also is yours; the world and all that is in it*
3 Or *and to your children yet to be*; Compare Psa 78:5-6 - *teach to their children, that the next generation might know them, the children yet unborn*
4 Compare Psa 119:103 - *sweet are your words to my taste, sweeter than honey*

Blessed are all those who walk in the way of righteousness
    and do not sin as the sinners during the days of the year:
when the sun crosses the heavens,
    entering and departing the passageways for thirty days
with the heads of thousands of the order of the stars,
    together with the four *inserted days* that are evenly spaced
and separate between the four portions of the year,
    that go before them and enter with them four days.

5   Because of these *inserted days*, men will make errors
    by not totaling them into the whole calculation of the year.
Yes, men will be to blame, and will not recognize them accurately.

6   For they belong in the total of the year,
    and are truly recorded forever,
one in the first passageway, one in the third,
    one in the fourth, and one in the sixth.
And the year is completed in 364 days.

Uriel and the Heavenly Lights

7   The account of *the stars* is accurate,
    and the recorded total is exact.
For the heavenly lights, the months, the festivals,
    the years, and the days
were shown and given to me by Uriel,
    whom the Lord of all creation ordered to explain to me the
        host of the heavens.

8   He has power over night and day in the heavens
    to cause the light to give light to men—sun, moon, and stars,
    and all the powers of the heavens that revolve in their
        circular chariots.

9   These are the orders *given* to the stars for their places during
        their seasons, festivals, and months.

10   These are the names of those who lead them,
         who watch that they enter at their times,
      in their orders, in their seasons, in their months,
         in their periods of dominion, and in their positions.
11   Entering first are the four leaders who divide the four parts
                     of the year,
         and after them the twelve leaders of the orders who divide
                     the months.
      For the 360 *days* there are heads over thousands who divide the
                     days;
         for the four inserted days there are the leaders that separate the
                     four parts of the year.
12   These heads over thousands are inserted between leader
                     and leader,
         each behind a station, but their leaders make the division.
13   These are the names of the leaders
         who divide the four established parts of the year:
      Melkel, Helemmelek, Meliyal, and Narel.[1]
14   And the names of those who lead them:
      Adnarel, Iyasusael, and Elomeel—
      these three follow the leaders of the orders,
         and there is one that follows the three leaders of the orders
      that follow the leaders of stations that divide the four parts of
                     the year.
15   In the beginning of the year, Melkeyal rises first and rules, who
                     is named the southern sun.
         The total days of his dominion while he bears rule are ninety-
                     one days.[2]
16   These are the signs of the days
         that will be seen on earth in the days of his dominion:

---

1 These four are over the four seasons of the year. Under each of these are
three leaders who preside over the three months of each season.
2 from spring to summer = 91 days under the dominion of Melkeyal

sweat, heat, and anxiety;
    all the trees bear fruit,
leaves are produced on all the trees,
    there is the harvest of wheat,
the *blooming of* garden-flowers,[1]
        and *the blooming of* all the flowers that come out in the field,
    but the trees of the winter season become withered.

17 These are the names of the leaders under them:[2]
    Berkael, Zelsabel, and another—
    added as a leader of a thousand—called Heloyalef.
The days of dominion of this *leader* then come to an end.

18 The next leader after him is Helemmelek,
    named the shining sun,
    and all the days of his light are ninety-one days.[3]

19 These are the signs of *his* days on the earth:
    glowing heat and dryness,
the trees prepare their fruits
    and produce all their fruits ripe and ready,
the sheep pair and become pregnant,
    all the fruits of the earth are gathered in, everything that is
            in the fields, and *everything in* the winepress.
    These things take place in the days of his dominion.

20 These are the names, the orders, and the leaders of those heads of
            thousands: Gedaeyal, Keel, and Heel,
    and the name of the head of a thousand which is added to
            them, Asphael.
The days of dominion of this *leader* then come to an end.

---

1 Or *rose-flowers*; Roses are not in the Hebrew Old Testament and only show up
in later examples of the Hebrew and Aramaic. Likely later alteration.
2 *the leaders under them* - the leaders of the three months.
3 The period from summer to autumn

6 ENOCH

Dream Visions

A Dream of the Great Flood

83 NOW, MY son Methuselah, I will show you all the visions I have seen by describing them to you.

2 I saw two visions before I married my wife,[1]
and the one *vision* was very different from the other:
the first when I was learning to write;
the second before I married your mother—
when I saw a terrible vision.
I prayed to the Lord about *these visions*.

3 I was lying down in the house of my grandfather, Mahalalel,[2]
and I saw a vision that the heavens collapsed, were removed,
and fell to the earth.

4 When it fell to the earth,
I saw how the earth was swallowed up in a great *watery* abyss,
mountains were suspended on mountains,
hills sank down on hills,
and high trees were pulled from their roots, fell down, and sunk
in the *watery* abyss.

5 Then a word came to my mouth.
I lifted up *my voice* to cry aloud, saying,
"The earth is destroyed."

---

1 Before the age of 65; See Gen 5:21 - *65 years, he fathered Methuselah*
2 See genealogy; Gen 5:15-18

6   My grandfather, Mahalalel woke me as I lay near him,
        saying to me, "Why are you crying, my son,
        and why are you wailing?"

7   I told him the whole vision that I saw,
        and he said to me, "A terrible thing you have seen, my son;
    the vision of your dream is potent,
        involving every secret sin of the earth:
    these sins must sink into the *watery* abyss
        and be destroyed with a great destruction.

8   Now, my son, arise and pray to the Lord of glory,
        for you are a believer.
    Pray that a remnant remains on the earth,
        and that He does not destroy the whole earth.

9   My son, this *judgment* will come on the earth from heaven,
        and great destruction will be on the earth."

10   After that I arose
        and prayed, petitioned, and pleaded.
    I wrote down my prayer
        for the generations of the world,
    and I will show everything to you,
        my son Methuselah.

11   I went out beneath *the sky* and gazed at the heavens.
    I saw the sun rising in the east
        and the moon setting in the west.
    I saw a few *scattered* stars, the whole earth,
        and everything as He established in the beginning.
    Then I blessed the Lord of judgment and praised Him,
        because He made the sun emerge from the windows of the east,
    so that *the sun* ascended, rising across the sky,
        and set out to pursue the path shown to him.[1]

---

1 i.e. the sun rose and crossed the sky as usual

Enoch's Prayer for Mercy

84 I LIFTED up my hands in righteousness,
blessed the holy and Great One,
and I spoke with the breath of my mouth.
  I spoke with the tongue of flesh
that God made for the children of men,
  that they should speak with it,
and gave them breath, the tongue, and the mouth,
  that they might speak with them.

2   "Blessed are you, O Lord King,
    great and mighty in Your greatness,
Lord of the whole creation of the heavens,
    King of kings and God of the whole world.
Your power, authority, and greatness last forever and ever,
    Your dominion throughout all generations.
All the heavens are Your throne forever,
    and the whole earth is Your footstool forever and ever." [1]

3   "For You have made and rule over all things,
    and nothing is too hard for You.
Wisdom does not leave the place of Your throne,
    nor turns away from Your presence.
You know, see, and hear everything;
    there is nothing hidden from You,
    for you perceive everything."

4   "Now the angels of Your heavens are guilty of sin,
    and Your wrath rests on the flesh of men
    until the great day of judgment.
5   Now, O God, Lord, and Great King,

---

1 Compare Isa 66:1 - *Heaven is my throne, and the earth is my footstool*

I beg and plead for You to answer my prayer,
  to leave me descendants on *the* earth.
Do not destroy all the flesh of man,
  or make the earth without inhabitant
  in eternal destruction.

6   Now, my Lord, destroy from the earth
       the flesh that has stirred up Your wrath,
     but with the flesh of righteousness and uprightness
       establish *them* as a plant of the eternal seed.
     Do not hide Your face
       from the prayer of your servant, O Lord."

A Dream of the History of the World from Adam

85

AFTER THIS, I saw another dream-vision,[1]
and I will describe the whole dream to you, my son.

2   Enoch lifted up *his voice* and spoke to his son Methuselah:
       My son, I will speak to you. Hear my words
       and listen to the dream-vision of your father.
3   Before I married your mother, Edna, I saw a vision while in bed,[2]
       and behold a bull came out of the earth.[3]
     That bull was white;
       and a heifer came after it[4] along with two bulls,
       one of them black, the other red.[5]
4   The black bull gored the red one
       and pursued him over the earth.
     Then I could no longer see the red bull.

---

1 Compare Dan 7:7 ISV - *night visions*
2 Compare Dan 7:1 ISV - *Daniel dreamed a dream, receiving visions in his mind
while in bed*
3 Adam; see Gen 2:7 - *the LORD God formed the man of dust from the ground*
4 Eve; see Gen 2:21-23 - *she shall be called Woman*
5 Cain and Abel; see Gen 4:1-2

5   But the black bull grew, and a heifer went with him,
        and I saw that many oxen came from him
        that resembled and followed him.
6   That cow, the first one, left the first bull to find the red one,
        but did not find him,
        and cried with great sorrow as she sought him.
7   I watched until the first bull came to her, comforting her,
        and from that time onward she cried no more.
8   After that, she gave birth to another white bull.
        After him, she gave birth to many bulls and black cows.
9   In my sleep, I also saw that white bull growing,
        and it became a great white bull,
        and many white bulls came from him that resembled him.
    They gave birth to many white bulls that resembled them,
        one following the other, very many.

Fallen Angels and Giants Plague Mankind

86

AGAIN, I looked closely[1] as I slept.
I surveyed the heavens above, and behold,
a star fell from heaven![2]
        It arose, ate, and pastured among those oxen.
2   After that, I saw the large black oxen,
        and behold, they all exchanged their stalls, their pastures,
                and their *fellow* cattle,
        and began to live with each other.
3   Again I was watching the vision,
        and looked towards the heavens, and behold,
        I saw many stars descend![3]

---

1 Or *saw with my eyes*
2 Either Azazel or Samyaza; see Enoch 88:1, 10:4; Compare Rev 9:1 - *a star
fallen from heaven to earth*; Luk 10:18 - *I saw Satan fall like lightning from heaven*
3 *many stars*: the other fallen angels. See Enoch 6:6

These cast themselves down from heaven to that first star.
They became bulls among those cattle,
>   pasturing with them and among them.
4   I watched, observing them,
>   and behold, they all acted like horses in heat,
>   and began to approach the young cows.
Those all became pregnant
>   and gave birth to elephants, camels, and donkeys.[1]
5   All the oxen were alarmed and terrified by them,
>   and *the elephants, camels, and donkeys* began biting with
>>   their teeth, devouring, and goring with their tusks.
6   They also devoured those oxen.
And behold, all the creatures[2] of the earth trembled,
>   shaking before them as they fled.

The Coming of Seven Angels

87 AGAIN, I saw how they gored each other and devoured one another.
And the earth cried aloud.
2   I raised my eyes again to heaven and saw the vision,
>   and behold! beings came down from heaven
>   who were like men of pure white.[3]
Four went out from that place,
>   then three *more* with them.
3   Those three *white figures* that came down after *them*
>   grasped me by my hand and took me up—
away from the generations of the earth,

---

1 *elephants*: Titans; *camels*: Nephilim; *donkeys*: Eliud; Three kinds of giants mentioned in Enoch 7:2
2 Or *children*
3 seven angels; See Enoch 20:1-8; Compare Rev 8:2 - *the seven angels who stand before God*

raised me up to a lofty place,
    showed me a tower raised high above the earth,
        and all the hills were lower.
4   One *white figure* said to me,
        "Stay here until you see everything that happens
    to those elephants, camels, and donkeys,
        and the stars, the oxen, and all of them."

The Punishment of the Fallen Angels

88 I SAW one of the four *white figures* who came out first.
He seized that first star that fell from heaven,
    bound it hand and foot, and cast it into a valley.
        Now that valley was narrow and deep, horrible and dark.
2   One of the *white figures* drew a sword
        and gave it to those elephants, camels, and donkeys.
    So, they began to strike each other,
        and the whole earth quaked because of them.
3   As I watched the vision, behold,
        one of the four *white figures* hurled stones from heaven,
    gathered all the great stars,
        took those who chased like horses in heat,
    bound them all hand and foot,
        and cast them into a cavity of the earth.[1]

The Flood and the Deliverance of Noah

89 ONE OF the four *white figures* went to one of the white
bulls[2] and taught it a mystery.
    It was born a bull but became a man.

---

1 Compare Psa 36:12 - *There, those who do evil have fallen; They have been thrown down, and they cannot get up.*
2 Noah

That man constructed a vessel. He lived in it,[1]
    three bulls lived with him in that vessel,
    and they were closed in.[2]

2   Again, I raised my eyes to heaven and saw a high roof
    with seven water gates on it,
    and its torrents flowed with abundant water.[3]

3   I looked again, and behold,
    fountains [4] opened on the surface of the land.
Water began to swell, rising in the animal pens.
I watched until all the pens were underwater;

4   the water, darkness, and mist increased on it.
As I watched the water level,
    the water rose above the heights, spilling over,
    and it stood upon the earth.

5   All the cattle gathered together
    until I saw how they sank, were swallowed up
    and perished in the water.

6   But the vessel floated on the water,
    while all the oxen, elephants, camels, and donkeys
sank to the bottom with all the animals
    so that I could no longer see them.
They were unable to escape,
    perishing as they sank into the depths.

7   Again, I beheld the vision
    until those water gates closed on the high roof,
and the fountains of the earth were closed,
    while other depths were opened.

---

1 The ark; Compare Gen 6:14,17; 7:1 - *Make yourself an ark of gopher wood...
Noah did this... Then the LORD said to Noah, "Go into the ark, you and all your
household*
2 Compare Gen 7:16 - *And the LORD shut him in*
3 Compare Gen 7:11-12 - *the windows of the heavens were opened. And rain fell
upon the earth forty days and forty nights*
4 Compare Gen 7:11 - *the fountains of the great deep burst forth*

8   Then the water ran down into these *depths*,
      until the earth became visible.
The vessel settled on the earth,
      the darkness retired, and light appeared.
9   Then the white bull that became a man
      came out of that vessel and his three bulls with him:
one of the three was white like that bull,
      one was red as blood, and one black.
And that white bull departed from them.

From the Death of Noah to the Exodus

10   They brought out beasts of the field and birds,
      and from them came a wide variety of kinds:
lions, tigers, wolves, dogs, hyenas, wild boars, foxes,
      squirrels, swine, falcons, vultures, kites, eagles,
          and ravens.
And a white bull was born among them.[1]
11   They began to bite one another.
That white bull born among them begat a wild donkey[2]
      and a white bull,[3]
and the wild donkeys multiplied.
12   This *white* bull that was born from *a white bull*
      fathered a wild black boar and a white sheep.[4]
The *wild boar* fathered many boars,
      and the sheep fathered twelve sheep.
13   When those twelve sheep were grown,
      they gave up one of their own to the donkeys.[5]

---

1 Abraham
2 Ishmael; see Gen 16:12 - *He shall be a wild donkey of a man*
3 Isaac
4 Esau and Jacob (or Israel); see Psa 79:13 - *the sheep of your pasture*
5 Joseph to the Midianites (Arabs)

The donkeys then gave up this sheep to the wolves,[1]
  and that sheep grew up among the wolves.

14 The Lord brought the eleven sheep to live with *the one*,
  to pasture with it among the wolves.
  And they multiplied, becoming many flocks of sheep.

15 The wolves began to fear them;
  they oppressed *the sheep*
  until they destroyed their little ones.
  The wolves cast *the sheep's* young into a river of high water,
  and the sheep cried aloud for their little ones,
  complaining to their Lord.

16 A sheep that was rescued[2] from the wolves fled,
  escaping to the wild donkeys.
  I saw the *flock of* sheep, how they lamented and cried,
  praying to their Lord with all their might,
  until the Lord of the sheep heard their cry,
  came down from His high dwelling,
  went to them, and pastured them.

17 He called the *one* sheep that escaped the wolves
  and spoke with it about the wolves,
  telling it to warn *the wolves* to leave the *flock of* sheep untouched.

18 That sheep went to the wolves according to the word of the Lord,
  and a *second* sheep[3] met the *first sheep*, going with it.
  The two went, entering together into the assembly of the wolves
      and spoke with them,
  warning them not to touch the sheep from then on.

19 After that, I saw the wolves,
  how they highly oppressed the *flock of* sheep with their power,
  and the sheep *all* cried aloud.

20 The Lord came to the *two* sheep,

---

1 *wolves*: Egyptians
2 Moses
3 Aaron

and they began to smite the wolves.[1]
The wolves expressed their torment,
    but the sheep immediately stopped crying, and became quiet.

21   I watched the sheep as they departed from among the wolves;
    but the eyes of the wolves were blinded to it.
Then the wolves left, chasing the sheep with all their might.

22   The Lord of the sheep went with *the flock*, leading them,
    and all his sheep followed him.
His face was dazzling, glorious, and terrible to behold.[2]

23   Yet the wolves chased after the sheep,
    until they reached a sea of water.[3]

24   The sea was divided,
    the water stood before *the sheep* on either side,
and their Lord led them,
    placing Himself between them and the wolves.[4]

25   When the wolves could no longer see the sheep,
    they went into the midst of the sea;
the wolves following the sheep,
    running after them into the sea.

26   As *the wolves* beheld the Lord of the sheep,
    they turned to escape from His presence,
but the sea gathered itself together,
    and returned to its original state.
The water swelled, rising until it covered the wolves.

27   I saw that all the wolves who chased the sheep
    drowned and perished.

---

1 The plagues of Egypt
2 Compare Exo 13:21-22 ISV - *The LORD went in front of them... a pillar of fire*
3 The Red Sea
4 Compare Exo 14:19-20 ISV - *the angel of God... moved behind them... one side did not come near the other*

The Wilderness, the Law, and the Promised Land

28 But the *flock of* sheep passed over the water,
    and went out into a wilderness
    where there was no water and no grass.
  Their eyes were opened, and they began to see.
  I saw the Lord of the sheep pasturing them,
    giving them water, and grass.
  The *head* sheep went *with them*, leading them.

29 The *head* sheep climbed to the top of a high rock,
    until the Lord of the sheep sent him back to *the flock.*[1]

30 After that, I saw the Lord of the sheep standing before them,
    His appearance great, terrible, and majestic.
  All the sheep saw Him
    and were afraid before His face.

31 They all feared and trembled because of Him.
  With the second sheep[2] among *the flock*,
    they all cried out to the *head* sheep,
  "We are not able to stand before our Lord or to behold Him."

32   The head sheep climbed again to the top of the rock.
  The *flock of* sheep were blinded,
    wandering from the path shown to them by the *head sheep*,
    but he was unaware.

33 The Lord of the sheep was very angry with them.
  The *head* sheep discovered all this, went from the top of the rock
      down to the sheep,
    and found many of them blinded and straying.

34 Those who saw him feared and trembled at his presence,
    and longed to return to their folds.

35 The *head* sheep took other sheep with it,
    came to those that had fallen away, and killed them.

---

1 Moses' ascent of Sinai and return to Israel at God's command, Exo 19.
2 Aaron

And the sheep feared the *head* sheep's presence.

Thus that sheep brought back those that had fallen away,
>and they returned to their folds.

36 I beheld this vision until that sheep became a man,
>built a house for the Lord of the sheep,
>and placed all the sheep in that house.[1]

37 I saw the *second* sheep—that met the head sheep—fall asleep.[2]

I watched until all the great sheep perished,
>and little ones arose in their place.

They came to a pasture and approached a stream of water.[3]

38 Then the head sheep that had become a man
>withdrew from them and fell asleep.

All the sheep searched for him[4]
>and cried bitterly because of him.

39 I watched until they stopped crying for that sheep
>and crossed that stream of water.

There arose two sheep as leaders[5]
>to replace all the leaders that had fallen asleep.

40 I saw the sheep come to a good place,
>a pleasant and glorious land,
>and behold those sheep were satisfied.

And that house stood among them in the pleasant land.

Time of the Judges Until the Temple

41 Sometimes their eyes were opened, and sometimes blinded,
>until another *lead* sheep arose and led them,[6]

---

1 made the tabernacle the center of their worship
2 Death of Aaron
3 The Jordan River
4 They could not find the body. Compare Jude 1:9 ISV - *the archangel Michael, when he argued with the devil and fought over the body of Moses*
5 Joshua and Caleb
6 Samuel

bringing them all back as their eyes were opened.

42 The dogs, foxes, and wild boars[1] began devouring the sheep
until the Lord of the sheep raised up another sheep:
a ram from among them to lead them.[2]

43 That ram struck the sides of the dogs, foxes, and wild boars
until he destroyed many.

44 The *lead* sheep whose eyes were opened
watched the ram among the sheep,[3]
until *the ram* abandoned the way of the Lord
and began to butt the *flock of* sheep,
trampling on them and behaving shamefully.

45 The Lord of the sheep sent the *lead* sheep to a lamb,[4]
raising it to become a ram and the leader of the sheep[5]
instead of the ram that abandoned the way of the Lord.

46 *The lead sheep* went to *this lamb*,
spoke to it alone, raised it to being a ram,
and made it the prince and leader of the sheep;
but during all these things those dogs[6] oppressed the sheep.

47 The first ram pursued the second ram;
that second ram arose and fled before it;
and I watched until those dogs pulled down the first ram.

48 Now the second ram arose and led the little sheep.

49 Those sheep grew and multiplied,
and all the dogs, foxes, and wild boars feared,
fleeing before the *second* ram,
because it butted and killed the wild beasts.
Those wild beasts no longer had power over the sheep,

---

1 *dogs:* Philistines; *wild boars:* Edomites; *foxes:* likely the Ammonites
2 King Saul
3 Samuel saw King Saul among the sheep
4 Or *another sheep*
5 King David
6 *dogs:* Philistines

robbing nothing from them.

That ram begat many sheep and fell asleep.

Now a little sheep became a ram in its place,[1]

　　becoming prince and leader of those sheep.

50　That house became great and broad,[2]

　　and it was built for the sheep.

A tower, tall and great, was built on the house

　　for the Lord of the sheep.

The house was low, but the tower was tall and high.[3]

The Lord of the sheep stood on the tower,

　　and they offered a full table before him.[4]

Kingdoms of Israel and Judah, Destruction of Jerusalem

51　Again I beheld the sheep, how they went astray,

　　going many ways and leaving their house.

The Lord of the sheep called some from among the sheep[5]

　　and sent them to their *fellow* sheep,

　　but their *fellow* sheep killed them.[6]

52　One of them, *a ram*, escaped and was not killed.

　　It sped away[7] and cried aloud over the flock.

The *flock* hunted *that ram* to kill it,

　　but the Lord of the sheep saved it from them

　　and brought it up to me,[8] causing it to dwell there.

53　Many other sheep he sent to those sheep,

　　to testify to them and lament over them.

---

1 King Solomon
2 Compare Lev 10:6 - *your brothers, the whole house of Israel*
3 *house*: Jerusalem; *tower*: the temple
4 offerings and sacrifices
5 the prophets
6 Compare 1Ki 18:4 ISV - *Jezebel was trying to destroy the LORD's prophets*
7 Compare 1Ki 19:3 ISV - *Elijah... got up and ran for his life*
8 to Enoch; Compare 2Ki 2:11 - *Elijah went up by a whirlwind into heaven*

54   Afterward I saw that when they left the house of the Lord and His
          tower,

   they departed entirely, and their eyes were blinded.

I saw the Lord of the sheep,

   how He worked terrible slaughter among them in their herds,

   until those sheep invited that slaughter and betrayed

     the Lord's place.[1]

55   *The Lord of the sheep* gave them over into the hands of the lions,

          tigers, wolves, and hyenas,

   and into the hands of the foxes and to all the wild beasts.[2]

Those wild beasts tore the sheep to pieces.

56   I saw that *the Lord of the sheep* forsook their house and their tower

   and gave them all into the hand of the *tigers,*[3]

to tear and devour them,[4]

   and into the hand of every wild beast.

57   I began to cry aloud with all my power,

   to appeal to the Lord of the sheep,

to show Him what was happening to the sheep:

   that they were devoured by all the wild beasts.

58   But He remained unmoved though He saw it,

   and rejoiced when they were devoured, swallowed, and

     robbed,[5]

and left them in the hand of all the beasts to be devoured.

---

1 Ahaz calls in heathen nations. Compare 2Ki 16:7 ISV - *So Ahaz sent envoys to Tiglath-pileser, king of Assyria to tell him, "I am your servant and son. Save me from the king of Aram and the king of Israel, who are attacking me."*

2 *lions*: Assyrians; *tigers*: Babylonians; *wolves*: Egyptians; *hyenas*: perhaps Ethiopians or the Syrians; *foxes*: likely the Ammonites; *wild beasts*: other nations

3 Or *lions*; Meaning Babylonians; see Jer 39:1 - *Babylon... came against Jerusalem and besieged it*

4 *devour*; Compare Jer 12:9; Isa 56:9; Eze 34:5,8

5 Compare Jer 12:8,12 ISV - *My inheritance has become like a lion in the forest to me. She roars at me; therefore, I hate her... a sword of the LORD will devour from one end of the land to the other*

59   He called seventy shepherds[1] and reassigned the sheep to them
        so they could pasture them.
     He spoke to the shepherds and their subordinates,
        "Let each and every one of you pasture the sheep from now on,
        doing everything that I command you to do.
60   I will deliver them to you rightfully numbered
        and tell you which of them are to be destroyed—
        those you will destroy."
     And *the Lord of the sheep* gave the sheep over to *the shepherds.*
61   *The Lord of the sheep* called another and spoke to him,
        "Observe and record everything that the shepherds do to
                the sheep;
        for they will destroy more of them than I have commanded.
62   Write down every excess and destruction done by the shepherds,
        how many they destroy by My command,
        and how many they destroy by their own will.
     Record separately each destruction by each shepherd.
63   Number aloud in My hearing how many they destroy,
        and how many they deliver over for destruction.
     This will be my testimony against them,
        to recognize every deed of the shepherds,
     that I may consider and see what they do,
        whether or not they follow My command that I have
                commanded them.
64   But they will not know it,
        and you will not declare it to them, nor admonish them,
     but write down all the destruction of the shepherds,
        each one in its time,

---

1 *shepherds*: angels; Charles notes, "There may be some distant connection
between the seventy angels here and the seventy guardian angels of the Gentile
nations." See Deu 32:8 - *when he divided mankind, he fixed the borders of the peoples according to the number of the sons of God* (angels); Psa 82:1-8 - *God has taken
his place in the divine council; in the midst of the gods* (angels) *he holds judgment*

and lay everything before Me."

65 As I looked, those shepherds pastured in their season.
   They began to destroy, slaying more than they were instructed,
      and they delivered the sheep into the hand of the lions.[1]

66 The lions and tigers[2] ate, devouring the majority of the sheep,
      and the wild boars[3] ate along with them.
   They burned the tower and demolished the house.[4]

67 I became greatly distressed over that tower
      because the house of the sheep was demolished,
   and I was then unable to see if the sheep entered the house.

Destruction of Jerusalem to the Return from Captivity

68 The shepherds[5] and their associates handed over the sheep
      to all the wild beasts to devour them.
   Each one of them received in his time a fixed number.
   The other[6] wrote it in a book:
      how many of the sheep each one of them destroyed.

69 Each one killed, destroying many more than was commanded,
      and I wept, lamenting over the sheep.

70 Thus in the vision, I saw the one who was writing,
      how he daily wrote down everyone the shepherds destroyed.

---

1 Compare Eze 34:8-10 - *my sheep have become food for all the wild beasts...
because my shepherds have not searched for my sheep, but the shepherds have fed
themselves, and have not fed my sheep, therefore, you shepherds, hear the word of
the LORD: Thus says the Lord GOD, Behold, I am against the shepherds, and I will
require my sheep at their hand and put a stop to their feeding the sheep.*

2 *lions*: Assyrians; *tigers*: Babylonians

3 *wild boars*: Edomites; Compare Eze 25:12 - *Edom acted revengefully against the
house of Judah*; Psa 137:7

4 Compare Jer 52:12-13 - *Nebuzaradan the captain of... Babylon, entered Jerusalem. And he burned the house of the LORD, and the king's house and all the houses of
Jerusalem*

5 *shepherds*: angels; see note on Enoch 89:59

6 *the other*: the archangel Michael

He brought up, opened, and showed this whole book to the
      Lord of the sheep: everything they had done,
  all that each of them took away,
  and all they handed over to destruction.

71   The book was read before the Lord of the sheep,
  and *the Lord of the sheep* took the book from his hand
  and read it, sealed it, and laid it down.[1]

The Time of Cyrus to Alexander the Great

72   At once, I saw how the shepherds[2] pastured for twelve hours,
  and behold three of those sheep turned back[3]
  and made the journey until they entered in,
  and began to build up all that had fallen down of that house.
  Wild boars[4] tried to hinder them, but they were unable.

73   The *sheep* resumed building as before;
  they raised up that tower;
  and it was named the high tower.
  They again placed a table before the tower,
  but the bread on it was polluted and impure.

74   So the eyes of the sheep were blinded;
  they did not see, and neither did their shepherds.
  Therefore, the *sheep* were given over to the shepherds for great
      destruction;
    the shepherds trampled the sheep with their feet
      and devoured them.

75   The Lord of the sheep remained steadfast
  until all the sheep were scattered over the field

---

1 Compare Dan 12:4 - *seal the book, until the time of the end*
2 *shepherds*: angels; see note on Enoch 89:59
3 Zerubbabel, Joshua, and either Ezra or Nehemiah
4 *wild boars*: The Samaritans

and mingled with *the beasts*, and *the shepherds* did not save
them out of the hand of the beasts.

76 The one writing the book carried it up and presented it,
read it before the Lord of the sheep and pleaded with Him,
begging Him on their behalf, as he read to Him all that the
shepherds had done,
and gave testimony before Him against all the shepherds.

Then the *writer* took the book itself,
laid it down beside *the Lord of the sheep,*
and departed.

Alexander the Great to the Greco-Syrian Domination

90 I OBSERVED, during this time, that thirty-five[1] shepherds[2]
were pasturing this way.
They all served out their time like the first *shepherd* did.
Others then received the *sheep* into their hands
to pasture them for their appointed time,
each shepherd for his own term of service.

2 Afterward, I saw in my vision, all the birds of heaven coming:
the eagles, vultures, kites, and ravens.[3]
Now the eagles led all the birds.
The *birds* devoured the sheep—pecking out their eyes and
devouring their flesh.

3 The sheep cried out because their flesh was being devoured by
the birds.
As for me, in my sleep, I was distressed from watching the
shepherd who pastured the sheep.

---

1 Or *37*; the number 37 is an apparent manuscript error. 35 is the sum of the
two periods of shepherds already dealt with (12+23). See also verse 5
2 *shepherds*: angels; see note on Enoch 89:59
3 *eagles*: Greeks or Macedonians; *vultures & kites*: Egyptians; *ravens*: Syrians

4   I saw the sheep devoured by the dogs, eagles, and kites.[1]
       They left neither flesh nor skin nor sinew remaining on the *sheep*
              until only their bones remained;[2]
       their bones fell to the earth, and the sheep became few.

5   I watched until twenty-three[3] *shepherds* had served out their
              pasturing,
       completing their term of service fifty-eight times.

Greco-Syrian Domination to the Maccabean Revolt

6   Behold, small lambs were born to those white sheep,
              and they opened their eyes to see, crying out to the sheep.

7   Yes, *the lambs* cried to them, but *the sheep* did not listen to their
              words.
       They were exceedingly deaf, and their eyes were exceedingly
              blinded.

8   I saw in the vision how the ravens[4] swarmed the lambs,
              taking one of them.
       The ravens dashed *many of* the sheep to pieces and devoured
              them.[5]

9   As I watched, the lambs grew horns,
              but the ravens cast those horns down.
       I observed until one of the sheep sprouted a great horn,[6]
              and the *horned lambs* had their eyes opened.

10   *The great horned sheep* pastured with[7] the *flock*, and their eyes
              opened.

_____

1 *dogs*: Philistines; *eagles*: Greeks or Macedonians; *kites*: Egyptians
2 Compare Mic 3:2-3 - *evil, who tear the skin from off my people and their flesh
from off their bones, who eat the flesh of my people, and flay their skin from off them,
and break their bones in pieces*
3 (35+23=58); See also verse 1: (12+23+23=58)
4 *ravens*: Syrians
5 Syrians attack Israel and kill Onias III, 171 B. C.; see 2 Macc 4:33-35
6 Judas Maccabeus
7 Or *looked at*

It cried to the sheep,

the rams saw it,

and all ran to it.

11 Despite all this, the eagles, vultures, ravens, and kites kept tearing
the sheep,

swooping down on them, and devouring them.

Still the sheep remained silent,

but the rams lamented and cried aloud.

12 The ravens fought, battling against *the great horned sheep*

and sought to lay low its horn,

but they had no power over it.

Last Assault of the Unrighteous [1]

13/16[2] I watched as the shepherds, eagles, vultures, and kites[3] came;

they gathered together with the ravens[4]

to break the horn of *the great horned sheep*.

They battled, fighting with it;

and the great horned sheep battled with them

and cried out for help to come *rescue them*.

19 Then I saw a great sword was given to the sheep.

The sheep moved against all the beasts of the field to slay them,

and all the beasts and the birds of the heavens fled before their

faces.

14/17[5] I beheld that man,

who wrote in the book

according to the command of the Lord,

---

1 This section required reconstruction. Verses were out of order and duplicated
before the manuscripts were first numbered.

2 Verse 16 is a repeat of 13 - manuscript error

3 *vultures and kites*: may stand for Ammon and Edom

4 *ravens*: Syrians

5 Verse 17 is a repeat of 14 - manuscript error

until he opened the book about the destruction
 that the last twelve shepherds had done.
That man established in the presence of the Lord of the sheep
 that these *twelve shepherds* had destroyed much more
 than the shepherds that came before them.

15/18[1] I saw as the Lord of the sheep came to them,
 took in his hand the staff of his wrath,
 and struck the earth.
The earth broke open,
 and all the beasts and all the birds of the heavens
fell from among those sheep,
 were swallowed up in the earth,
 and it covered them.[2]

Judgment of Fallen Angels, the Shepherds, and Apostates

20 I watched as a throne was placed in the pleasant land,
 and the Lord of the sheep sat Himself on it.
The other[3] took the sealed books
 and opened those books before the Lord of the sheep.[4]

21 The Lord called to those men—
 the first seven who were *pure* white,[5]
and commanded them
 to bring before Him *the stars*,
beginning with the first star that led the way[6]

---

1 Verse 18 is a repeat of 15 - manuscript error
2 Compare Num 16:32-33 - *the earth opened its mouth and swallowed them up...
and the earth closed over them*
3 *the other*: the archangel Michael
4 Compare Dan 7:9-10 ISV - *the Ancient of Days was seated... The court sat in
judgment, and record books were unsealed.*
5 See Enoch 87:2; seven angels; See also Enoch 20:1-8; Compare Rev 8:2 - *the
seven angels who stand before God*
6 Either Samyaza or Azazel; Compare Enoch chapters 6, 9:6-7, and 86.

of all the stars who mated like horses.[1]

And they brought them all before Him.

22   He spoke to the man who wrote in His presence,

one of the seven *men of pure* white,

saying to him,

"Seize those seventy shepherds

to whom I delivered the sheep,

and by their own authority

slew more than I commanded them!"

23   Behold they were all bound;

I witnessed it as they all stood before Him;

24   the judgment was first held over the stars.

They were judged, found guilty,[2] and sent to the place of
condemnation.

They were cast into an abyss full of fire and roaring flames,

and filled with pillars of fire.[3]

25   Those seventy shepherds[4] were judged, found guilty, and cast
into that fiery abyss.[5]

26   I saw at that time how a similar gulf to the abyss opened

in the midst of the earth, full of fire.[6]

They brought those blinded sheep,

they were all judged and found guilty,

cast into the fiery abyss,

and they burned.

Now this abyss was to the right of that house.[7]

---

1 Fallen angels; See Enoch 86:3-4
2 Compare Job 25:5 - *the stars are not pure in his eyes*
3 Compare Rev 14:10 - *tormented with fire and sulfur in the presence of the holy
angels and in the presence of the Lamb*
4 *shepherds*: angels; see note on Enoch 89:59
5 Compare Mat 25:41 - *the eternal fire prepared for the devil and his angels*
6 Gehenna, the valley of Hinnom; See Mat 10:28 WEB - *Rather, fear him who is
able to destroy both soul and body in Gehenna.*
7 *to the right*: to the south of Jerusalem

27   And I saw those sheep burning;
> yes, their very selves.[1]

New Jerusalem, Conversion of the Nations, Resurrection of the Righteous, the Messiah

28   I stood to see as they folded up that old house,
> and carried off all the pillars.
>All the beams and ornaments of the house
> were simultaneously folded up with it.
>They carried it off
> and laid it in a place in the south of the land.

29   I watched until the Lord of the sheep brought a new house,[2]
> greater and higher than the first,
> and set it in the place of the first *house* that was folded up.
>All its pillars were new; its ornaments were new
> and larger than those of the first *house*, the old one he had
>   taken away;
> and all the sheep were in *the new house*.

30   I saw all the sheep that were left,
> all the beasts on the earth,

---

1 Or *and their bones burning*; Compare Isa 66:24 - *"And they shall go out and look on the dead bodies of the men who have rebelled against me. For their worm shall not die, their fire shall not be quenched, and they shall be an abhorrence to all flesh."*

2 The removal of the old Jerusalem and the setting up of the New Jerusalem. This expectation is derived from Old Testament prophecy: Eze chapters 40-48; Isa 54:11-12 - *I will set your stones in antimony, and lay your foundations with sapphires. I will make your pinnacles of agate, your gates of carbuncles, and all your wall of precious stones*; Isa 60; Hag 2:7-9 ISV - *The glory of this present house will be greater than was the former*; Compare Rev 21:2, 18-21 - *I saw the holy city, new Jerusalem, coming down out of heaven from God... The wall was built of jasper, while the city was pure gold, like clear glass. The foundations of the wall of the city were adorned with every kind of jewel. The first was jasper, the second sapphire, the third agate, the fourth emerald, the fifth onyx, the sixth carnelian, the seventh chrysolite, the eighth beryl, the ninth topaz, the tenth chrysoprase, the eleventh jacinth, the twelfth amethyst. And the twelve gates were twelve pearls, each of the gates made of a single pearl, and the street of the city was pure gold, like transparent glass.*

and all the birds of the heavens,

    falling down in public reverence to those sheep,

making requests of them,

    and obeying them in everything.

31   After that, those three clothed in white[1] took hold of me—

    who had seized me by the hand before when they took me up.

And the hand of that ram[2] also grabbed hold of me.

They took me up and set me among those sheep

    before the judgment took place.

32   Those sheep were all white;

    their wool was abundant and clean.[3]

33   All that had been destroyed and dispersed,

    all the beasts of the field,

and all the birds of the heavens,

    assembled in that house.

The Lord of the sheep rejoiced with great joy

    because all of them were good

    and had returned to His house.

34   I watched as they laid down the sword

    that had been given to the sheep.

They brought it back into the house,

    and it was sealed before the presence of the Lord.

All the sheep were invited into the house,

    but it could not hold them.

35   All their eyes were opened,

    and they saw good things.

There was not one among them that did not see.

36   I saw that the house was large, broad, and very full.

---

1 3 angels; See Enoch 87:2-3

2 *that ram*: Elijah; See Enoch 89:52

3 Compare Rev 7:13-14 - *clothed in white robes... made them white in the blood of the Lamb*

37 I saw that a white bull[1] was born with large horns;

all the beasts of the field and all the birds of the air feared him[2]

and made requests of him continually.

38 I watched as all their generations were transformed,

and they all became white bulls.

The first among them became a lamb,

that lamb became a great animal,

and had great black horns on its head.[3]

The Lord of the sheep rejoiced over it

and over all the oxen.

39 I slept among them,

and I awoke and saw everything.

40 This is the vision that I saw while I slept.

I awoke, blessed the Lord of righteousness,

and gave Him glory.

41 Then I wept with great weeping.

My tears were unending

until I could not stand it.

As I watched, they flowed because of what I saw.

For everything will come and be fulfilled.

All the deeds of men,

and the order in which they will happen,

were shown to me.

42 On that night, I remembered the first dream,

and because of it I wept and was troubled—

because I had seen that vision.

---

1 The Messiah; Compare 1 Co 15:45 - *Thus it is written, "The first man Adam became a living being"; the last Adam became a life-giving spirit*; See Enoch 85:3

2 Compare Rev 12:5 - *who is to rule all the nations with a rod of iron*

3 Compare Rev 5:6 - *among the elders I saw a Lamb standing... with seven horns and with seven eyes*

7 ENOCH

The Epistle of Enoch

Final Triumph Over Sin[1]

91

THE BOOK written by Enoch—
(Enoch indeed wrote this complete doctrine of wisdom,
praised by all men and a judge of all the earth)
    for all my children who will dwell on the earth.
And for the future generations
    who will follow moral virtue and peace.

2   Do not let your spirit be troubled because of the times;
    for the holy and great one has appointed days for all things.[2]

3   The Righteous One will arise from sleep,[3]
    shall arise and walk in the paths of righteousness,
    and His ways and words will be carried out

---

1 Chapters 91-93 required extreme reconstruction by Charles. They have been renumbered in the Enoch MSV for ease of reading and reference. The manuscripts were ordered as follows: 92; 91:1-10, 18-19; 93:1-10; 91:12-17; 93:11-14; 94; For the Modern Standard Version, chapter 92 became 91; 91:1-10, 18-19 became 92; 91:12-17 became 93:11-16; and 93:11-14 became 93:17-20; the previous 91:11 was created by a transcriber as an attempt to fix these problems and has been removed in the MSV.

2 Compare Ecc 3:1-22 ISV - *There is a season for everything, and a time for every event under heaven*

3 Resurrection of the Messiah; Compare 1 Co 15:4 - *he was raised on the third day*; Resurrection as waking from sleep: John 11:11-14 - *"Our friend Lazarus has fallen asleep, but I go to awaken him."... Now Jesus had spoken of his death, but they thought that he meant taking rest in sleep*; Mat 9:18, 23-25 - *"My daughter has just died"... "the girl is not dead but sleeping"*

in eternal goodness and grace.

4   He will be gracious to the righteous and give him eternal
        uprightness.
He will give him power,
    so that he will be endowed with goodness and righteousness;
    and he will walk in eternal light.

5   Sin will perish in darkness forever,
    and will not be seen again from that day forever more.

Enoch's Admonition to His Children

9 2 "NOW, MY son Methuselah, call your brothers to me,
        and bring to me all your mother's sons.
Because the word calls me,
    and the spirit is poured out on me,
so that I may show you everything
    that will happen to you forever."

2   After that Methuselah went,
        summoned all his brothers to him,
        and assembled his relatives.

3   He spoke to all the children of righteousness, saying,
    "Hear, you sons of Enoch, all the words of your father,
        and listen closely to the voice of my mouth;
for I caution you earnestly
    and say to you, beloved:
    love uprightness and walk in it.

4   Do not approach moral virtue with a double heart,[1]
        and do not associate with those who have a false heart.
But my sons, walk in righteousness,
    it will guide you on good paths,
    and righteousness will be your companion.

---

1 Compare Psa 12:2 - *with flattering lips and a double heart they speak.*

5   For I know that violence must increase on the earth.

Then a great reprimand will be carried out on the earth,[1]
    and all unrighteousness will come to an end.

Yes, *the earth* will be cut off from its roots,
    and its whole structure will be destroyed.

6   But unrighteousness will again take place on the earth.

    All the deeds of unrighteousness, violence, and transgression
        will abound twofold.

7   When all kinds of deeds increase with sin, unrighteousness,
        blasphemy, and violence,

    and apostasy, transgression, and uncleanness increase—

a great rebuke will come from heaven on all these.

The holy Lord will come out with wrath and chastisement
    to execute judgment on the earth.

8   In those days, violence will be cut off from its roots,

    unrighteousness and deceit from their roots;
    they will be destroyed from under heaven.

9   All the idols of the heathen will be abandoned,

    and their temples burned with fire;
    they will remove them from the whole earth.

The *idol worshipers* will be cast into the judgment of fire.

They will perish in wrath and in terrible judgment forever.

10   The righteous will arise from their sleep;[2]

wisdom will arise, and *she will* be given to them."

11   "Now I tell you, my sons, and show to you
    the paths of righteousness and the paths of violence.

Yes, I will show them to you again,
    so you will know what will come to pass.

---

1 The great flood; Compare Gen 7 - *the waters of the flood came upon the earth*
2 Compare 1Th 4:16 - *the Lord himself will descend from heaven with a cry of command... And the dead in Christ will rise first;* Dan 12:2 - *many of those who sleep in the dust of the earth shall awake, some to everlasting life*

12   Now, listen to me, my sons,

      and walk in the paths of righteousness.

   Do not walk in the paths of violence;

      for all who walk in the paths of evil will perish forever."

The Prophecy of Weeks

93
   AFTER THIS, Enoch gave his word,
   saying,

2   "Concerning the children of righteousness,

      the elect of the world,

   and the plant of uprightness;[1]

      I will speak these things.

   Yes, I, Enoch, will declare to you, my sons

      according to what appeared to me in the heavenly vision,

   which I have known through the word of the holy angels,

      and have learned from the heavenly tablets."

3   Enoch recounted from the books, saying,

      "I was born the seventh in the first week,[2]

      while judgment and righteousness still endured.[3]

4   After me, in the second week, great wickedness will arise;[4]

      deceit will spring up,

      and in *that week* will be the first end.[5]

   During *that end,* a man will be saved;

      at its ending, unrighteousness will grow up,

---

1 *plant of uprightness*: Israel; See Enoch 10:16, 62:8, 84:6, 93:5,10
2 Compare Gen 5:4-19 (Genealogy); Jude 1:14 - *Enoch, the seventh from Adam*
3 Or *were held back*; meaning uncertain
4 According to Enoch 6:6, 106:13 The fallen angels descended in the days of Jared, nearly 60 years before Enoch was born. This likely means that it took several decades or longer for the angelic corruption to spread to all mankind.
5 The great flood

and a law[1] will be made for the sinners.

5   After that, at the close of the third week,
      a man will be chosen as the plant of righteous judgment,
    and his inheritance[2] will become the plant of righteousness[3]
          forever more.

6   After that, at the close of the fourth week,
      visions of the holy and righteous will be seen,
    as well as a law for all generations;[4]
      and an enclosure will be made for them.

7   After that, at the close of the fifth week,
      the house of glory and dominion will be built to endure.

8   After that, in the sixth week,
      all who live then will be blinded,[5]
    and all their hearts will godlessly forsake wisdom.
    In *that week* a man will ascend.[6]
    At *that week's* close, the house of dominion will be burned with
          fire;
      and the whole race of the chosen root will be scattered.[7]

9   After that, in the seventh week,
      an apostate generation will arise.
    Its deeds will be many,
      and all its deeds will be apostate.

10 At the close *of the seventh week,*
      the elect will be chosen to spread the witness of righteousness
    from the eternal plant of righteousness,

---

1 Compare Gen 8:21, 9:17 - *God said to Noah, "This is the sign of the covenant that I have established between me and all flesh that is on the earth."*
2 Compare Gen 17:4-5 - *"Look, I've made a covenant with you. You will be the father of many nations... Abraham"*
3 *plant of righteousness*: Israel; See Enoch 10:16, 62:8, 84:6, 93:2,10
4 The law given on Sinai. *for all generations*: See Mat 5:18 - *(nothing) will pass from the Law until all is accomplished.*
5 The time of the divided kingdom of Israel
6 Elijah
7 Destruction of the Temple, and the nation carried into captivity

and to receive sevenfold instruction
concerning all His creation.

11 After that, there will be another week,
the eighth week—that of righteousness.
A sword will be given to *that week*
so that a righteous judgment can be executed on the oppressors;
sinners will be delivered into the hands of the righteous.

12 At *the week's* close, they will acquire houses through their
righteousness,
and a house will be built for the Great King
in glory forever more.

13 All mankind will look to the path of moral virtue.
Then, in the ninth week,
the righteous judgment will be revealed to the whole world.
All the works of the godless will vanish from all the earth,
and the world will be marked down for destruction.

14 After this, in the tenth week—in the seventh part,
there will be the great eternal judgment,
when He will execute vengeance among the angels.

15 The first heaven will depart and pass away;
a new heaven will appear;
and all the powers of the heavens will give sevenfold light.

16 After that there will be many weeks without number forever.
All will remain in goodness and righteousness,
and sin will not be mentioned again forever." [1]

The Lord is Beyond Understanding[2]

17 For who is there of all the children of men

---

1 Compare Isa 65:17 - *New heavens... former things shall not be remembered*
2 The translators agree that verses 17-20 (formerly 93:11-14; see footnote at beginning of chapter 91) do not belong in this book (7 Enoch, The Epistle of Enoch). These verses were likely from another part of the Book of Enoch.

that can hear the voice of the Holy One without being troubled? [1]

    Who can think his thoughts? [2]

Who is there that can behold all the works of heaven,

18   and how should anyone be able to view the heavens?

Who could understand the things of heaven,

    see a soul or a spirit and tell about it,

ascend to see all their ends,

    or think on them or do like them?

19   Who is there of all men that could know

        what is the breadth and the length of the earth,

    and to whom has been shown the measure [3] of all of them?

20   Or is there anyone who could discern the length of the heavens [4]

        or how great is their height, and on what are they founded,

    or how great is the number of the stars, and where do all the

        luminaries rest?

Enoch's Admonitions to the Righteous [5]

94 "NOW I say to you, my sons,

        love righteousness and walk in it;

for the paths of righteousness are worthy of acceptance,

    but the paths of unrighteousness will suddenly be

        destroyed and vanish.

2   To certain men of a generation,

        the paths of violence and death will be revealed.

They will distance themselves from those paths

    and will not follow them.

---

1 Compare Psa 29; Job 37:4-5; Exo 20:19 - *do not let God speak to us, lest we die*

2 Compare Isa 55:8 - *For my thoughts are not your thoughts*

3 Compare Job 38:4-5 - *"Where were you when I laid the foundation of the earth? Tell me, if you have understanding. Who determined its measurements*

4 Compare Jer 31:37- *Thus says the LORD: "If the heavens above can be measured... then I will cast off all the offspring of Israel*

5 Continuing from Ch 92 & 93:1-16; Enoch addressing his sons.

3   Now I say to you, the righteous:
    do not walk in the paths of wickedness,
nor in the paths of death,[1]
    and do not go near them, or you will be destroyed.
4   But seek and choose for yourselves both righteousness
         and the life of the chosen.
Walk in the paths of peace,
    and you will live and prosper.
5   Hold onto my words in your secret thoughts,
    and do not remove them from your hearts.
For I know that sinners will tempt men to pervert wisdom,
    so she[2] will find no place to stay,
    and temptations of every kind will not cease."

Woes for the Sinners

6   "Woe to those who build unrighteousness and oppression
    and lay deceit as a foundation.
For they will be suddenly overthrown,
    and will have no peace.
7   Woe to those who build their houses with sin.[3]
    For they will be overthrown from all their foundations,
        and they will fall by the sword.
Those who acquire *bribes of* gold and silver
        in *exchange for* their judgment will suddenly perish.
8   Woe to you, those who are rich,
    for you have trusted in your riches.[4]
You will be separated from your riches,

---

1 Compare Psa 1:1 - *Blessed is the man who walks not in the counsel of the wicked,*
nor stands in the way of sinners, nor sits in the seat of scoffers
2 The Holy Bible refers to wisdom as feminine. See Pro 8; Mat 11:19
3 Compare Jer 22:13 - *Woe to him who builds his house by unrighteousness*
4 Compare Pro 11:28 - *Whoever trusts in his riches will fall*

because you have not remembered the Most High
in the days of your riches.

9 You have committed blasphemy and unrighteousness,
and have been made ready for the day of slaughter,
the day of darkness, and the day of the great judgment.

10 Thus I speak and declare to you:
He who created you will overthrow you;
there will be no compassion over your fall;
your creator will rejoice at your destruction.[1]

11 In those days, your righteous men and women
will be an insult to the sinners and the godless."

Enoch's Grief

95 "OH THAT my eyes were a spring of water[2]
that I might weep over you,
and pour down my tears like mist.
Then I could rest from my troubled heart!

2 Who has permitted you to practice hatred and wickedness?
So, judgment will overtake you, sinners.

3 Do not fear the sinners, you righteous,
for the Lord will again deliver them into your hands,
for you to execute judgment on them as you desire.

4 Woe to you who declare curses[3] that cannot be undone.

---

1 Compare Deu 28:63 - *the LORD will take delight in bringing ruin upon you and destroying you*; Psa 37:13 - *the Lord laughs at the wicked, for he sees that his day is coming*; **Author's note:** This is God's sense of justice. It is the will of God that none should perish; 2Pe 2:9 - *not wishing that any should perish, but that all should reach repentance*; Eze 18:23 ISV - *"I don't take delight in the death of the wicked, do I?" asks the Lord GOD. "Shouldn't I rather delight when he turns from his wicked ways and lives?"*; God delights in justice because he is holy, but he would rather delight in forgiveness and compassion.

2 Or *fountain of water*; Compare Jer 9:1 - *Oh, that my head were a spring of water, and my eyes a fountain of tears*

3 Magical practices and incantations

Therefore, healing will be far from you because of your sins.[1]

5　　Woe to you who repay your neighbor with evil;[2]

for you will be repaid according to your works.[3]

6　　Woe to you, lying witnesses,

and to those who unbalance injustice,

for you will perish suddenly.

7　　Woe to you, sinners, for you persecute the righteous;

for you will be delivered up and persecuted because of injustice,

and its burden will be heavy on you."

Blessed Hope of the Messianic Kingdom

96 "BE HOPEFUL, you righteous; for the sinners will suddenly perish before you.

You will have lordship over them

according to your will.

2　　In the day of tribulation for the sinners,

your children will mount up and rise like eagles,[4]

and your nest will be higher than the vulture's nest.[5]

You will *both* ascend and enter the crevices of the earth,[6]

and the unending clefts of the rock,

finding every hiding place as you pursue

like rock badgers do when they flee oppressors.

---

1 Compare Exo 15:26

2 Compare Pro 17:13 ISV - *The person who repays good with evil will never see evil leave his home*; Pro 24:29 - *Do not say, "I will do to him as he has done to me; I will pay the man back for what he has done."*; Rom 12:17 - *Repay no one evil for evil*

3 Compare Jdg 1:7 - *As I have done, so God has repaid me*

4 Compare Isa 40:31 - *they shall mount up with wings like eagles*

5 Compare Jer 49:16 ISV - *The terror you cause and the pride of your heart have deceived you. You who live in hidden places in the rocks, who hold on to the heights of the hill, although you make your nest high like the eagle, I'll bring you down from there," declares the LORD.*

6 The righteous pursue the sinners everywhere they would hide; Compare Isa 2:10 - *Go into the rocks! Hide in the dust to escape the terror of the LORD and to escape the glory of his majesty!*

And the sirens[1] will sigh because of you and weep.[2]

3   So fear not, you that have suffered.

For you will be given healing,

  a bright light will enlighten you,[3]

and you will hear the voice of rest from heaven.

4   Woe to you, the sinners,

  for your riches make you appear like the righteous,[4]

but your hearts convict you of being sinners.

This fact will be a testimony against you—

  as a memorial of *your* evil deeds.

5   Woe to you who devour the finest of the wheat,[5]

  drink wine in large bowls,[6]

and trample the poor with your might.[7]

6   Woe to you who drink water from every fountain,[8]

  for you will quickly shrivel and wither away,

because you have forsaken the fountain of life.[9]

7   Woe to you who work unrighteousness, deceit, and blasphemy.

They will be a memorial against you

---

1 Or *satyrs*; Or *like sirens they*; see following footnote and Enoch 19:2 note
2 This seems to indicate that the righteous will even pursue the sirens (woman/bird hybrid wives of the fallen angels) or the satyrs (goat demons); Alternatively, the sirens/satyrs are distressed by the pursuit from the righteous of the sinful. Both ideas suggest a connection between the sirens/satyrs and the sinners being pursued, which could imply the presence of giants (offspring of the sirens). Giants in the end times are perhaps suggested by Isa 13:3 LXX - *I give command, and I bring them: giants are coming to fulfill my wrath*
3 Compare Joh 1:4 - *In him was life, and the life was the light of men.*
4 Compare Pro 22:4 - *The reward for humility and fear of the LORD is riches and honor and life.*
5 This is meant for those the Lord chooses to reward. See Psa 81:16 - *But he would feed you with the finest of the wheat*; Also Psa 147:14
6 Drink heavily; Compare Amo 6:4-6 - *Woe to those... who drink wine in bowls*
7 Compare Isa 3:14-15 - *"It is you who have devoured the vineyard, the spoil of the poor is in your houses. What do you mean by crushing my people, by grinding the face of the poor?" declares the Lord GOD of hosts.*
8 Or *who drink water from every time*
9 Compare Jer 2:13 - *they have forsaken me, the fountain of living waters*

displaying your evil.

8   Woe to you, the mighty,
> who oppress the righteous with your strength.
> For the day of your destruction is coming."

"At that time,
> many good days will come to the righteous—
> > in the day of your judgment."

The Sinful Will Come to Shame

9 7   "BELIEVE, YOU righteous ones, that the sinners
> >   will come to shame
> and perish in the day of unrighteousness.

2   Understand, *you sinners*, that the Most High is mindful
> > of your destruction,
> and the angels in heaven rejoice over your destruction.

3   What will you do, you sinners?
> Where will you escape to on that day of judgment,
> > when you hear the voices of the righteous in prayer?

4   Yes, you have the same fate as those
> > that this word will be a testimony against:
> > 'You have been companions of sinners.'

5   In those days, the prayer of the righteous will reach the Lord,
> and the days of your judgment will come for you.

6   All the words of your unrighteousness
> will be read aloud before the Great Holy One.
> Your faces will be covered with shame,
> > and He will reject every work
> > that is grounded in unrighteousness.

7   Woe to you, the sinners,
> who live on the sea and on the dry land.

The memory of your evil
   is something the sea and the land hold against you.[1]

8   Woe to you who acquire silver and gold in unrighteousness
       and say, 'We have become wealthy with riches,
       have possessions, and have gained everything that we wanted.[2]

9   Now let us do what we planned,
       for we have gathered silver,
       and we have many workmen in our houses.
   Our granaries are full to the brim
       as if they were tanks of water.'

10 Yes, and like water your lies will flow away.
   For your riches will not remain,
       but will quickly leave you.
   For you gained all of it unrighteously,
       and you will be given over to a great curse."

The Pride and Foolishness of Sin

98 "NOW I swear to you, to the wise and to the foolish.
       For you will have many experiences on the earth.

2   For you men will put on more adornments than a woman,
       and more colored garments than a virgin:
   in royalty, in grandeur, in power,
       in silver, in gold, in purple,
   in splendor, and in food—
       they will be poured out like water.

3   Therefore they will have a lack of sound teaching and wisdom,
       and they will perish because of it—
   together with their possessions,
       and with all their glory and their splendor.

---

1 Compare Lev 18:28 - *lest the land vomit you out when you make it unclean*
2 Compare Rev 3:17 - *For you say, I am rich, I have prospered, and I need nothing,
not realizing that you are wretched, pitiable, poor, blind, and naked*; also Luk 12:19

In shame, in slaughter, and in great poverty,
  their spirits will be cast into the furnace of fire.

4   I have sworn to you, the sinners,
    as a mountain has not become a slave,
  and a hill does not become the handmaid of a woman,
    in the same way, sin has not been sent on the earth.[1]
  But man has created it himself,[2]
    and those who commit it fall under a great curse.

5   The inability to bear children
    was not inflicted on a woman *by the Lord*,
  but because of the actions of her own hands
    she dies without children.[3]

6   I have sworn to you, the sinners, by the Holy Great One,
    that all your evil deeds are revealed in the heavens,
  and that none of your deeds of oppression are covered or hidden.

7   Do not think in your spirit nor say in your heart
    that you do not know or you do not see
  that every sin is recorded daily in heaven
    in the presence of the Most High.

8   From now on, you know that all your oppression
    that you use to oppress
    is written down daily until the day of your judgment.

9   Woe to you, the fools,
    for through your foolish practices, you will die.
  You commit evil against the wise,
    and so good things will not be yours.

---

1 Compare Jas 1:13 - *he should not say, "I am being tempted by God," because God cannot be tempted by evil, nor does he tempt anyone*
2 Compare Rom 5:12 - *Just as sin entered the world through one man, and death resulted from sin, therefore everyone dies, because everyone has sinned.*
3 The implication is that through righteous prayer, a barren woman can be healed. See Gen 17:17,19; 29:31; 30:22; 2Ki 4:16; Compare Jas 4:3-4 - *You do not have, because you do not ask. You ask and do not receive, because you ask wrongly, to spend it on your passions*

10 Now, be aware that you are prepared for the day of destruction.
    Why do you hope to live, you sinners?
But you will depart and die,
    for you have no ransom.[1]
You are prepared for the day of the great judgment,
    for the day of tribulation and great shame for your spirits.

11 Woe to you, those who have a hard heart,
    who work wickedness, and eat blood.[2]
Who is your source of good food, drink, and satisfaction?
The Lord Most High has placed all these good things in
        abundance on the earth—
    therefore you will have no peace.

12 Woe to you who love the deeds of unrighteousness.
    Why do you hope for good things for yourselves?
Know that you will be delivered into the hands of the righteous.
They will cut off your necks, slay you,
    and have no mercy on you.

13 Woe to you who rejoice in the tribulation of the righteous,
    for no grave will be dug for you.

14 Woe to you who give no value to the words of the righteous,
    for you will have no hope of life.

15 Woe to you who write down lying and godless words,
    for they write down their lies for men to hear,
    and act godlessly towards *their* neighbor.

16 Therefore, they will have no peace
    but will die a sudden death."

---

1 Jesus is the ransom for believers; See 1Ti 2:6 - *who gave himself as a ransom for all*
2 Compare Lev 17:10; Deu 12:23 WEB - *Only be sure that you don't eat the blood; for the blood is the life.*

Woes Pronounced on the Godless

99

"WOE TO you who work godlessness,
who give honor and glory to lies.

You will die; you will not have a happy life.

2   Woe to them who pervert the words of moral virtue,
broke the eternal law,
and transform themselves into what they were not.[1]
They will be trampled underfoot on the earth.

3   In those days, make ready, you righteous,
to raise your prayers as a memorial,[2]
and place them as a testimony before the angels,[3]
that they may place the sin of the sinners
for a memorial before the Most High.

4   In those days, the nations will be unsettled.
The families of the nations will arise
on the day of destruction.

5   In those days, the poor will go out
and carry their children with them.
And they will abandon them,
thus their children will die by their hand.
Yes, they will abandon their little babies,
and not return to them,
and will have no pity on their beloved ones."

---

1 Charles notes that this indicates a medical procedure. Compare Gen 10:8 LXX - *(Nimrod): he began to be a giant upon the earth*; Or the KJV - *Nimrod: he began to be a mighty one in the earth*; The word 'began' is chalal, which means *a desecration* on a ritual level or genetic level. 'Giant' or 'mighty one' is gibbor, which can mean an offspring of the Nephilim/descended from fallen angels. Tom Horn states in Apollyon Rising 2012: "Therefore, in modern language, this text could accurately be translated to say: *'And Nimrod began to change genetically, becoming a gibborim, the offspring of watchers on earth.'*"
2 Compare Psa 141:2 - *Let my prayer be counted as incense before you, and the lifting up of my hands as the evening sacrifice!*
3 Compare Rev 8:3-4 - *the prayers of the saints, rose before God from the hand of the angel*

6   "Again I swear to you, the sinners,

     that sin is prepared for a day of unending bloodshed.

7   Those who worship stones,

     and carved images of gold, silver, wood, stone, and clay,

and those who worship impure spirits and demons,[1]

     and all kinds of idols worshiped through ignorance:

     these will give you no help.

8   They will become godless,

     deceived by their own hearts.[2]

They will their eyes will be blinded

     through fearful hearts,

     and through visions in their dreams.[3]

9   Through these, they will become godless and fearful.

For within a lie, they will carry out all their work,

     and will worship a stone.

Therefore, they will perish in an instant.

10   But in those days, blessed are all those

     who accept the words of wisdom, understand them,

and observe the paths of the Most High,

     walk in the path of His righteousness,

and do not become godless with those

     who are already without God.

For *the righteous* will be saved.

11   Woe to you who spread evil to your neighbors,

     for you will be slain in Sheol.

12   Woe to you who make deceitful and false measures,[4]

     who cause bitterness on the earth.

---

1 Compare Lev 17:7 - *they shall no more sacrifice their sacrifices to goat demons;*
2 Compare Jer 17:9 - *The heart is deceitful above all things, and desperately sick*
3 Compare Deu 13:1-3 - *a dreamer of dreams arises among you... if he says, 'Let us go after other gods,'... you shall not listen to the words of... that dreamer of dreams*
4 Compare Pro 11:1 ISV - *The LORD hates false scales, but he delights in accurate weights;* Amos 8:5; Hos 12:7 ISV - *Now as for the merchant, deceitful balances remain in his hand, and he loves to defraud*

For by these things, you will be utterly consumed.

13   Woe to you who build your houses
      through the grievous toil of others.[1]

All your building materials
    are the bricks and stones of sin.

I tell you that you will have no peace.

14   Woe to them who reject both the standards
      and eternal heritage of their fathers,
        whose souls follow after idols.

For they will have no rest.

15   Woe to them who work unrighteousness,
      help oppression, and slay their neighbors
        until the day of the great judgment.

16   For He will cast down your glory,
      bring affliction on your hearts,

arouse His righteous anger,
    and destroy you all with the sword.

All the holy and righteous
    will remember your sins."

Sinners Destroy Each Other

100 "DURING THOSE days,
in one location, the fathers will be struck down
        with their sons,

and brothers, one with another, will fall in death
    until the streams flow with their blood.

2   For a man will not withhold his hand
      from slaying his sons and his sons' sons,

and the sinner will not withhold his hand
    from his honored brother,

---

1 Compare Jer 22:13 - *Woe to him who builds his house by unrighteousness... who makes his neighbor serve him for nothing*

from dawn until sunset they will slay one another.

3   The horse will walk breast deep in the blood of sinners,[1]
and the chariot will sink in to its height.

4   In those days, the angels will descend into the secret places
and gather together in one place all those
who brought down *their* sin.
The Most High will arise on that day of judgment
to execute great judgment among sinners.

5   Over all the righteous and holy,
He will appoint guardians from among the holy angels
to guard them as the apple of His eye,[2]
until He makes an end of all wickedness and all sin.
And though the righteous sleep a long sleep,[3]
they have nothing to fear."

6   "The children of the earth will see the wise secure,[4]
will understand all the words of this book,
and recognize that their riches will not save them
during the overthrow of their sins.[5]

7   Woe to you, sinners, on the day of great suffering,
you who afflict the righteous and burn them with fire.
You will be repaid based on your works.

8   Woe to you, the hard hearted,[6]

---

1 Compare Rev 14:20 ISV - *blood flowed from the wine press as high as a horse's bridle for about 183 miles*

2 Compare Deu 32:9-10 - *the LORD's portion is his people... he kept him as the apple of his eye*

3 Compare 1Th 4:14 - *through Jesus, God will bring with him those who have fallen asleep*

4 Compare Pro 10:9 - *Whoever walks in integrity walks securely*

5 Compare Jer 18:23 WEB - *Don't blot out their sin from your sight, Let them be overthrown before you*

6 Compare Rom 2:5 ESV - *But because of your hard and impenitent heart you are storing up wrath for yourself on the day of wrath when God's righteous judgment will be revealed.*

who watch and plan wickedness.
Therefore, fear will come over you,
and there will be none to help you.

9   Woe to you, the sinners,
because of the words of your mouth.
Because of the work of your hands,
that your godlessness brought about,
you will burn in blazing flames
that burn worse than fire.

10 Now, be aware that He will ask about your deeds
from the angels in heaven.[1]
From the sun, from the moon, and from the stars
He will ask about your sins,
because on the earth, you execute judgment on the righteous.

11 He will summon to testify against you
every cloud, mist, dew, and rain.
For they will all be withheld from falling because of you,[2]
and they will be aware of your sins.

12 Now give gifts to the rain,[3]
so it will not be withheld from falling on you,
and also to the dew—once you pay gold and silver
it may descend.

13 When the frost and snow bring their chill,
and all the snowstorms with all their plagues fall on you,
in those days, you will be unable to stand before them."

---

1 God often asks questions to which he already knows the answer. See Gen 3:9
- *the LORD God called to the man and said to him, 'Where are you?'*; Gen 4:9 - *Then
the LORD said to Cain, "Where is Abel your brother?"*; Gen 18:9 - *"Where is Sarah
your wife?'*
2 Compare Jer 5:24-25 - *rain in its season... Your iniquities have turned these
away*
3 Verse 12 is spoken ironically; The Holy Bible uses irony many times, such as
1Ki 18:27 ISV - *"Shout louder! He's a god, so maybe he's busy. Maybe he's relieving
himself."*

The Fear of the Lord

101

"CONSIDER THE heavens, you sons of men,
and every work of the Most High,
and fear working evil in His presence.

2 If He closes the windows of heaven,
and withholds the mist and the dew from falling on the earth
because of you,[1]
what will you do then?

3 If He sends His anger on you because of your deeds,
you cannot petition Him.[2]
For you spoke proud and insolent words against His righteousness,
therefore, you will have no peace.

4 Do you not see the ship captains,
how the waves toss their vessels back and forth,
how the winds shake them,
and cause them great trouble?

5 Therefore, they fear,
because all their valuables go out to sea with them.
In their hearts they have dark fear
that the sea will swallow them, and they will die there.

6 Are not the entire sea and all its waters,
and all its movements, the work of the Most High?
Has He not set limits to its striving,
and confined it throughout by the sand?[3]

---

1 Compare 1Ki 17:1;18:18 - *Elijah... said to Ahab, "As the LORD, the God of Israel, lives, before whom I stand, there shall be neither dew nor rain these years, except by my word."... because you have abandoned the commandments of the LORD*
2 Compare Isa 59:2 - *your sins have hidden his face from you so that he does not hear*; Psa 66:18 - *If I had cherished iniquity in my heart, the Lord would not have listened*; 1Sa 8:18 - *the LORD will not answer you in that day*
3 Compare Job 38:8-11 ISV - *Who enclosed the sea with limits... a boundary for it... and said, 'You may come only this far and no more. Your majestic waves will stop here.'?*

7   At His rebuke, it is afraid and dries up,[1]
        and all its fish die and all that is in it;[2]
        but you sinners on the earth do not fear Him.

8   Has he not made the heavens and the earth,
        and all that is in them?[3]
    Who has given understanding and wisdom to everything
        that moves on the earth and in the sea?

9   Do not the sailors of the ships fear the sea?
        Yet sinners do not fear the Most High."

The Fates of the Righteous and the Unrighteous

102 "IN THOSE days,
    when He brings a grievous fire on you,
        where will you escape to, and where will you find deliverance?
    When He launches His word against you
        will you not be frightened and fearful?

2   All the stars will be frightened with great fear,
        all the earth will be fearful,
        and tremble and be alarmed."

3   "All the kings[4] will execute their commands
        and try hiding themselves from the presence of
            the Great Glory.[5]

---

1 Compare Nah 1:4 - *He rebukes the sea and makes it dry*
2 Compare Psa 105:29 - *He turned their water into blood, so that the fish died*
3 Compare Psa 146:5-6 - *the God of Jacob... who made heaven and earth, the sea, and all that is in them*
4 Or *angels*
5 Compare Rev 6:15-16 - *Then the kings of the earth and the great ones and the generals and the rich and the powerful, and everyone, slave and free, hid themselves in the caves and among the rocks of the mountains, calling to the mountains and rocks, "Fall on us and hide us from the face of him who is seated on the throne, and from the wrath of the Lamb*; Gen 3:8 - *the man and his wife hid themselves from the presence of the LORD God among the trees of the garden*

The children of *the* earth will tremble and quake;
>   you sinners will be cursed forever;
>   you will have no peace.

4 Do not fear, you souls of the righteous;
>   be filled with hope
>   you that have died in righteousness.

5 Do not grieve if your soul descended into death *1* with sorrow,
>   or that your fleshly life did not reflect your good deeds.*2*

But how much worse would have been the day you became
>   sinners—
>   *once you were* in the day of cursing and punishment.

6 Yet when you die, the sinners speak over you,
>   'As we die, so the righteous die,
>   and what benefit do they gain for their actions?

7 Behold, even as we die,
>   they also die in grief and darkness.
>   What more do they have than us?
>   From now on we are equal.

8 What will they receive,
>   and what will they see forever?
>   Behold, they have died also.
>   From now on and forever they will not see light.'

9 I tell you, the sinners, you are content to eat, drink, rob, sin, strip
>   men naked, acquire wealth, and see good days.

10 Have you seen the righteous—how their end turns out,
>   that no kind of violence is found in them until their death?

11 'Yet still they perished,

---

1 lit. *Sheol*; Also in verse 11; Charles notes at this time period the term "Sheol" sometimes meant the shared waiting place of the afterlife, not just the destination of sinners. Compare Job 30:23 WEB - *you will bring me to death, to the house appointed for all living*

2 Compare Luk 16:25 - *you in your lifetime received your good things, and Lazarus in like manner bad things; but now he is comforted here, and you are in anguish*

and it is as if they never lived.
Their spirits descended into death in suffering.'"

Considering a Holy or Sinful Life

103

"THEREFORE I swear to you, the righteous,
by the glory of the Great One,
who is honored and mighty in dominion;
by His greatness I swear to you."

2   "I know a mystery
and have read the heavenly tablets,
and saw the holy books.
I found *the righteous* written in them,
and this was inscribed about them:
3   that all goodness, joy, and glory are prepared for them,
and written down for the spirits of those
who die in righteousness.
And that abundant goodness will be given to them
in reward for their labors,
and that their inheritance far exceeds the inheritance of the
living.
4   The spirits of you that died in righteousness
will live and rejoice.[1]
Their spirits will not perish,
nor will the memory *of them* pass away from the presence of the
Great One
even unto all the generations of the world.
Why should you fear their humiliation?"

5   "Woe to you, the sinners, when you die.

---

1 Compare Mar 12:27 - *He is not God of the dead, but of the living*

If you die in the wealth of your sins,
>   and those who are like you say about you,
>   'Blessed are the sinners—they have seen all their days.

6   They died in prosperity and in wealth
>   and have not seen tribulation or murder in their lives.
>   They died in honor,
>   and judgment was not executed on them during their lives.'

7   Be aware that their souls are sent down into Sheol,
>   and they will be wretched in their great tribulation."

8   "Your spirits will enter into darkness and chains,
>   where there is a burning flame and terrible judgment.
>   The great judgment will be for all the generations of the world.
>   Woe to you, for you will have no peace."

Warning of Speaking Against the Righteous

9   "Do not say *this* about the righteous
>   and those who are good in life:
>   'In our troubled days we did backbreaking work,
>   experienced every trouble, were met with great evil,
>   were consumed, have become few, and our spirits *made* small.

10   We have been destroyed and found no one to help us
>   even with a word.
>   We have been tortured and destroyed,
>   and did not hope to see life from day to day.

11   We hoped to be the head and have become the tail.[1]
>   We worked extremely hard and had no satisfaction in our labor.
>   We have become food for the sinners and the unrighteous,
>   and they have laid their yoke heavily on us.

12   Those that hated and struck us have dominion over us.

---

1 Compare Deu 28:13 - *the LORD will make you the head and not the tail*

We bowed our necks to those that hated us,
> but they did not pity us.

13 We desired to get away from them
> that we might escape and be at rest,

but found no place to run away to that was safe from them.

14 We complained to the rulers in our tribulation,
> and cried out against those who devoured us,

but they did not attend to our cries
> and would not listen to our voices.

15 They helped those who robbed us and devoured us
> and those who made us few.

They concealed their oppression,
> and did not remove the yoke of those
> who devoured us, scattered us, and murdered us.

They concealed their murder, and did not remember
> that they had lifted up their hands against us.'"

Assurance for the Righteous

104
"I SWEAR to you, that in heaven the angels remember you for *your* good before the glory of the Great One,[1]

and your names are written before the glory of the Great One.

2 Be hopeful—for previously you were put to shame through evil
> and affliction;

but now you will shine as the lights of heaven.

You will shine, you will be seen,
> and the gateways of heaven will be opened to you.

3 In your outcry, call for judgment, and it will appear to you.

For all your troubles will be inflicted on the rulers,
> and on anyone helping those who robbed you.

4 Be hopeful, and do not cast away your hopes.

---

1 Compare Mat 18:10 - *do not despise one of these little ones. For I tell you that in heaven their angels always see the face of my Father who is in heaven*

For you will have great joy like the angels of heaven.[1]

5   What will you be required to do?
You will not have to hide on the day of the great judgment;
    you will not be found as sinners.
The eternal judgment will be far from you
    for all the generations of the world.

6   Now fear not, you righteous,
    when you see the sinners growing strong
    and prospering in their ways.
Do not ally with them—keep away from their violence.
    For you will be companions of the hosts of heaven.

7   Although you sinners say,
    'All our sins will not be discovered and written down,'
    still they will write down all your sins every day.

8   Now I show to you:
    that light and darkness, day and night,
    see all your sins.

9   Do not be godless in your hearts, and do not lie.
Do not change the words of truth,
    or distort the words of the Holy One,
    or meditate on your idols.
For all your lying and all your godlessness
    do not result in righteousness
    but in great sin."

10   "Now, I know this mystery,
    that sinners will alter and pervert the words of righteousness in
        many ways,
and will speak wicked words, lie, practice great deception, and
        write books about their own words.

---

1 Compare Luk 15:10 ISV - *there is joy in the presence of God's angels*

11   If only they would write down truthfully all my words,
        and not change or diminish anything from my words,
     but write them all down truthfully—
        all that I first testified concerning them.
12   Now, I know another mystery:
        that books will be given to the righteous and the wise
        to become a source of joy, moral virtue, and great wisdom.
13   The books will be given to them,
        they will believe in them, and rejoice over them.
     Then the righteous,
        who have learned the paths of moral virtue from those books,
     will be rewarded."

Preach to Mankind

105

"IN THOSE days," says the Lord,
     "Summon the children of the earth
        and testify wisdom over them.[1]
     Show them—for you are their guides,
        that the whole earth will be reordered.[2]
2   For I and my Son[3] will be united with them forever
        on the path of holiness in their lives,[4]
     and you will have peace."
     Rejoice, you children of truth. Amen.

---

1 Compare Rev 14:6 - *I saw another angel flying overhead with the eternal gospel
to proclaim to those who live on earth—to every nation, tribe, language, and people.*
2 Compare Isa 11:6-10 - *The cow and the bear shall graze; their young shall lie
down together; and the lion shall eat straw like the ox. The nursing child shall play
over the hole of the cobra... They shall not hurt or destroy... for the earth shall be full
of the knowledge of the LORD*; 2Pe 3:10-13 - *we are looking forward to new heavens
and a new earth, where righteousness is at home*
3 Compare 1John 5:5 - *Jesus is the Son of God*
4 Compare Isa 35:8 - *a highway shall be there, and it shall be called the Way of
Holiness; the unclean shall not pass over it*

8 ENOCH

Methuselah

The Birth of Noah

106 AFTER A time, my son Methuselah took a wife for his son Lamech,

and she became pregnant by Lamech and bore a son.

2   His flesh was white as snow and red as the blooming of a flower;*1*

the hair of his head was white and curly like wool,

and his eyes were beautiful.

When he opened his eyes, he lit up the whole house like

the sun,*2*

and the whole house was filled with light.

3   When he was taken from the hand of the midwife,

he opened his mouth and praised the Lord.*3*

4   His father, Lamech, was afraid of him and fled,

and went to his father, Methuselah.

5   He said to him, "I have fathered a unique son,

different from humans and unlike them—

resembling the sons of the angels of heaven.

His nature is different; he is not like us.

---

1 Or *rose*; Note the word *rose* was not in early Hebrew or Aramaic. Likely later alteration. Also verse 10.

2 Compare Exo 34:30 - *the people of Israel saw Moses, and behold, the skin of his face shone, and they were afraid to come near him*

3 Compare Exo 34:29 - *Moses did not know that the skin of his face shone because he had been talking with God*

His eyes are like the rays of the sun,
   and his face is glorious.[1]

6   I'm thinking he is not from me, but from the angels.
      And I fear that during his life something extraordinary will
         happen on the earth.[2]

7   Now, my father, I am here to urgently plead with you
      to go to Enoch, our father, and learn the truth from him,
      for he lives among the angels."

8   When Methuselah heard the words of his son,
      he came to me at the ends of the earth—
      for he heard that I was there—and he cried aloud.[3]
   I heard his voice, and I came to him, saying,
   "Behold, here I am, my son,
      why have you come to me?"

9   He answered, saying,
      "I have come to you because of a great event,
      and I have approached because of a disturbing vision.

10 Now, my father, hear me:
      a child was born to Lamech, my son,
      and there is none like him.
   His nature is not like man's nature;
      the color of his flesh is whiter than snow
      and redder than the bloom of a flower.
   The hair of his head is whiter than white wool,

---

1 Compare Acts 6:15 - *his face was like the face of an angel*; In ancient times, Noah was seen as a type that prefigured the Messiah. Thus, the connotations of a divine birth. Just as Jesus was the second Adam, (1Cor 15:21-22,45-47) the Messiah was seen as the second Noah (savior and cleanser of the world). 2Pe 2:5 - *Noah, a herald of righteousness*; In 1 Peter chapter 3, the apostle Peter ties the ideas of Jesus and his sacrifice together with Noah, the flood, and baptism.
2 Biblically, we know Lamech viewed Noah's birth as extraordinary in some fashion, as he prophesied when naming the child in Gen 5:29 that Noah would bring an end to the curse God put over the land in Gen 3:17-19.
3 Not necromancy. Enoch never died, as stated in Heb 11:5 ISV - *Enoch was taken away without experiencing death*; Enoch 106:7 - *he lives among the angels*

and his eyes are like the rays of the sun.

He opened his eyes and lit up the whole house.

11 When he was taken from the hands of the midwife,

he opened his mouth and blessed the Lord of heaven.

12 His father, Lamech, was afraid and fled to me.

He did not believe that this was his child,

but thought *the child* looked like the angels of heaven.

Behold I have come to you

that you might show me the truth."

13 I, Enoch, answered, saying to him,

"The Lord will do a new thing on the earth.*1*

I saw this in a vision

and have already told you

that in the generation of my father, Jared,*2*

some of the powers*3* of heaven

violated the word of the Lord.

14 Behold, they commit sin, violate the law,*4*

and have united themselves with women.

They commit sin with them,

have married some of them,

and have fathered children by them.*5*

17*6* They produce giants on the earth,

---

1 Compare Isa 43:19 - *Behold, I am doing a new thing*; Also with regard to destruction: Num 16:30 - *But if the LORD creates something new, and the ground opens its mouth and swallows them up with all that belongs to them, and they go down alive into Sheol, then you shall know that these men have despised the LORD.*
2 *Jared*; Gen 5:18-20; The name Jared means *Shall come down*
3 Or *angels*; or *heights*; meaning uncertain
4 Compare Jude 1:6 - *the angels who did not stay within their own position of authority, but left their proper dwelling*
5 Compare Gen 6:2;4 ISV - *some divine beings noticed how attractive human women were, so they took wives for themselves... those divine beings were having sexual relations with those human women, who gave birth to children for them. These children became the heroes and legendary figures of ancient times.*
6 Verse order from Charles

not according to the spirit, but according to the flesh.

A great punishment will be on the earth,

and the earth will be cleansed from all impurity.

15 Yes, a great destruction will come over the whole earth.

There will be a flood and a great destruction for one year.

16 Your newborn grandson will be left on the earth,

and his three children will be saved with him.

When all mankind on the earth dies,

he and his sons will be saved.

18 Now tell your son, Lamech,

that the newborn is indeed his son,

and *to* name him Noah.

For he will be your inheritance.[1]

He and his sons will be saved

from the destruction that will come on the earth

because of all the sin and all the unrighteousness

that will take place on the earth in his days.[2]

19 After those days, unrighteousness will surpass what was first

committed on the earth.

For I know the mysteries of the holy ones.

For He, the Lord, showed me and informed me.

And I read *the mysteries* in the heavenly tablets."

Relief to Come

107 "I SAW written on *the heavenly tablets*

that generation upon generation will do evil,

until a generation of righteousness arises,

evil actions are destroyed,

---

1 Or *he will be left to you*

2 Compare Gen 6:5 - *The LORD saw that the wickedness of man was great in the earth, and that every intention of the thoughts of his heart was only evil continually.*

sin passes away from the earth,[1]
  and every aspect of good comes on *the earth*.

2 Now, my son, go and tell your son, Lamech,
  that his newborn son is truly his son—
  that is no lie."

3 When Methuselah heard the words of his father, Enoch,
  (for he showed him everything in secret)
he returned and informed *Lamech*,
  who named his son Noah.
For *Noah* will comfort the earth after all the destruction.[2]

A Message for Those in the Last Days

108 *THIS IS* another book that Enoch wrote for his son Methuselah and for those who come after him, who keep the law in the last days.

2 You who have done good will wait for the days
  when those who work evil are put to an end,
  and the might of the evildoer ends.

3 You indeed wait until sin passes away,
  for their names will be blotted out of the book of life and out
    of the holy books.
Their seed will be destroyed forever;
  their spirits will be routed.
They will cry and mourn in the lightless waste;

---

1 Compare Zec 14:9 - *And the LORD will be king over all the earth. On that day the LORD will be one and his name one.*
2 Noah's name means *to bring relief* or *comfort*; Removal of the curse on the ground. Compare Gen 5:29 - *and called his name Noah, saying, "Out of the ground that the LORD has cursed, this one shall bring us relief from our work and from the painful toil of our hands.";* Gen 3:17 - *cursed is the ground because of you;* Gen 8:20-21 - *Noah built an altar... the LORD said in his heart, "I will never again curse the ground because of man*

they will burn in the bottomless fire.

4   There I perceived, as it were,

a cloud that could not be seen through,

and because of its depth, I could not perceive its size.

I saw a flame of fire blazing brightly,

and things like shining mountains circling

and sweeping back and forth.

5   I asked one of the holy angels who was with me,

saying to him, "What is this shining thing?

for it is not heaven, but only the flames of a blazing fire,

and the voice of weeping, crying, lamentation, and great pain."

6   He said to me, "This place that you see—

the spirits of sinners and blasphemers are cast here,

and *the spirits* of those who work wickedness,

and of those who pervert everything the Lord has spoken

through the mouth of the prophets—

the things that are still to come.

7   For some of *the things to come* are written and inscribed above in

heaven, so the angels may read them[1]

to know what will befall the sinners, the spirits of the humble,

and *the spirits* of those who allowed their bodies to suffer and

were rewarded by God.

And *for the angels to read* of those who were put to shame by

wicked men:

8   who love God and loved neither gold nor silver[2]

nor any of the good things that are in the world,

but gave over their bodies to torture.

9   Who, since they were born, did not long after earthly food,

---

1 Many passages in the Holy Bible have books and scrolls in heaven; Zec 5:1
- *a flying scroll*; Rev 5:1 - *a scroll written within and on the back, sealed with seven
seals*; Rev 10:2 - *a little scroll open in his hand*; Eze 2:9 - *behold, a scroll of a book*;
Dan 12:1 - *written in the book*; Rev 21:27 KJV - *the Lamb's book of life*
2 Compare Mat 6:24 - *You cannot serve God and money*

but thought of everything as a passing breath,[1]
and lived that way.
The Lord tested them greatly;[2]
their spirits were found pure,
and they blessed His name.
10   All the blessings destined for them,
I have written in the books.
He has assigned them their reward,
because they were found to love heaven
more than their lives in the world." [3]

For the Lord Has Said,

"Though they were trampled by wicked men,
were abused and reviled by them,
and were put to shame,
yet they blessed Me.
11   Now, I will call the spirits of those who were righteous,
who belong to the generation of light,
and I will transform those who were found in[4] darkness—
who in the flesh were not repaid with the honor fitting for
their faithfulness.[5]

---

1 Compare Jas 4:14 - *What is your life? For you are a mist that appears for a little time and then vanishes*; Ecc 1:2 - *All is vanity*; The word for vanity is *hebel*, which means *mist* or *a passing breath*.
2 Compare Deu 13:1-3 - *For the LORD your God is testing you, to know whether you love the LORD your God with all your heart and with all your soul*; Pro 17:3 - *the LORD tests hearts*; Psa 11:5 - *The LORD tests the righteous*; Jer 17:10 - *"I the LORD search the heart and test the mind, to give every man according to his ways, according to the fruit of his deeds."*; Job 7:17-18 - *test him every moment*
3 Compare Heb 11:10-16 - *they desire a better country, that is, a heavenly one*
4 Or *were born to*
5 While salvation in the Holy Bible cannot be earned, (it is the free gift of God through Jesus Christ) rewards for righteousness and faithfulness are frequently discussed in both the Old and New Testaments.

12   I will bring out in shining light[1]
        those who love My holy name,
        and I will seat each on the throne of his honor."

13   They will shine for time without end;
        for righteousness is the judgment of God.
    To the faithful, He will give faithfulness
        as they live in paths of truth.
14   The righteous will then see
        those who remained in[2] darkness cast into darkness,
        while the righteous shine brilliantly.
15   The sinners will cry aloud
        and see them shining brilliantly.[3]
    The righteous will indeed go
        where eternity[4] awaits for them.

---

1 Compare Psa 104:2 - *covering yourself with light as with a garment*
2 Or *were born in*
3 Compare Psa 36:9 ISV - *in your light we will see light*; Dan 12:3 ESV - *those who are wise shall shine like the brightness of the sky above; and those who turn many to righteousness, like the stars forever and ever*
4 Or *days and seasons*

The End of the Book of Enoch

Reference

Parallel Passages

Commentary

God's Plan to Save You

PARALLEL PASSAGES

Enoch and the New Testament

The influence of Enoch on the New Testament has been greater than that of all the other apocryphal and pseudepigraphal books taken together. The evidence for this conclusion may for the sake of convenience be arranged under two heads:

1. A series of passages of the New Testament which either in phraseology or idea directly depend on or are illustrative of passages in Enoch.

2. Doctrines in Enoch which had an undoubted share in molding the corresponding New Testament doctrines.

The selection of passages here has been restricted to the New Testament because the Book of Enoch has been shown to predate the birth of Christ and the writings of the gospels. Footnotes throughout the MSV show vast connection in thought between this book and the writings of the Old Testament. Unlike these parallel passages here, the footnotes do not usually represent a direct relationship but instead demonstrate the consistency of ideas and themes between the Holy Bible and the Book of Enoch.

There are many other potential parallel passages between the Book of Enoch and the New Testament that have not been included in this section. The verses given are some of the more obvious parallels with clear connections. There would be ample material to fill entire books comparing the parallel passages not covered.

Unless otherwise indicated, all Scripture quotations are from the ESV Bible (The Holy Bible, English Standard Version).

Book of Enoch	*New Testament*
En 1:9 Behold, the Lord comes with ten thousands of His holy ones, to execute judgment on all, and to convict all the ungodly, and to convict all flesh of all the works of their ungodliness that they have ungodly committed, and of all the harsh things that ungodly sinners have spoken against Him.	**Jude 1:14-15** Enoch, the seventh from Adam, prophesied, saying, "Behold, the Lord comes with ten thousands of his holy ones, 15 to execute judgment on all and to convict all the ungodly of all their deeds of ungodliness that they have committed in such an ungodly way, and of all the harsh things that ungodly sinners have spoken against him."
En 5:7 But for the chosen there will be light, joy, and peace, and they will inherit the earth.	**Matt 5:5** Blessed are the meek, for they shall inherit the earth
En 9:4-5 And they said to the Lord of the ages, "Lord of lords, God of gods, King of kings, and God of the ages, the throne of Your glory *stands* unto all the generations of the ages, and Your name is holy, glorious, and blessed unto all the ages! 5 You have made all things, and You have power over all things. All things are naked and open in Your sight. You see all things, and nothing can hide itself from You."	**Rev 17:14; 19:16** Lord of lords and King of kings **Rev 4:11** "Worthy are you, our Lord and God, to receive glory and honor and power, for you created all things, and by your will they existed and were created." **Heb 4:13** And no creature is hidden from his sight, but all are naked and exposed to the eyes of him to whom we must give account.

Book of Enoch

En 10:11-13 And the Lord said to Michael, "Go, bind Samyaza and his associates who have united themselves with women... ¹² ...bind them fast for seventy generations in the valleys of the earth, until the day of their judgment and of their fulfillment, until the judgment that is forever and ever is consummated. ¹³ In those days, they will be taken to the abyss of fire, to *their* torment, and to the prison where they will be confined forever."

En 12:4 ...the *fallen* watchers of the heavens who have left the high heaven...

En 14:5 From now on, you will not ascend into heaven until all eternity. The order has been decreed beneath the earth to chain you for all the days of the world.

New Testament

Jude 1:6 ...the angels who did not stay within their own position of authority, but left their proper dwelling, he has kept in eternal chains under gloomy darkness until the judgment of the great day...

2Pe 2:4 God did not spare angels when they sinned, but cast them into hell and committed them to chains of gloomy darkness to be kept until the judgment.

Rev 20:10 ...the devil who had deceived them was thrown into the lake of fire and sulfur... and they will be tormented day and night forever and ever.

Jude 1:6 ISV ...angels who did not keep their own position but abandoned their assigned place.

Rev 20:1-3 Then I saw an angel coming down from heaven, holding in his hand the key to the bottomless pit and a great chain. ² And he seized... the devil and Satan, and bound him for a thousand years, ³ and threw him into the pit, and shut it and sealed it over him...

Book of Enoch	*New Testament*
En 19:1 ...lead them astray into sacrificing to demons as gods...	**1Co 10:20** ...what pagans sacrifice they offer to demons and not to God.
En 22:9,10 *(The angel Raphael addressing Enoch in the region of the dead)* This division was made for the spirits of the righteous... ¹⁰ This *division* was *also* made for sinners when they die...	**Luke 16:26** *(Abraham addressing a dead sinner from the region of the blessed)* Between us and you there is a great gulf fixed.
En 25:7,6 ⁷ Then I blessed the God of Glory, the Eternal King, who has prepared such things *(the tree of life)* for the righteous. *He* created them and promised to give to them.... ⁶ ...with its fragrance in their bones. They will live a long life on earth, such as your fathers lived in their days. No sorrow, plague, torment, nor calamity will touch them.	**Rev 22:2** ...on either side of the river, the tree of life with its twelve kinds of fruit, yielding its fruit each month. The leaves of the tree were for the healing of the nations. **Rev 2:7** To the one who conquers I will grant to eat of the tree of life, which is in the paradise of God. **Rev 22:14 KJV** Blessed are they that do his commandments, that they may have right to the tree of life...
En 38:2 ...where will those who denied the Lord of hosts find refuge? It would be better for them if they had not been born...	**Matt 26:24** ...woe to that man by whom the Son of Man is betrayed! It would have been better for that man if he had not been born.

Book of Enoch	New Testament
En 39:3-7 ...a whirlwind carried me off from the earth and set me down at the end of the heavens. ⁴ There I saw another vision: the dwellings of the saints... ⁵ ...with His righteous angels... ⁶ ...under the wings of the Lord of hosts... ⁷ Their lips praise the name of the Lord of hosts...	**2 Cor 12:1-4** ...visions and revelations of the Lord. ² I know a man in Christ... caught up to the third heaven—whether in the body or out of the body I do not know, God knows. ³ And I know that this man was caught up into paradise... ⁴ ...and he heard things that cannot be told, which man may not utter.
	Rev 19:1 ...heard what seemed to be the loud voice of a great multitude in heaven, crying out, "Hallelujah! Salvation and glory and power belong to our God...
En 39:13 ...those who do not sleep... and say...	**Rev 4:8** They have no rest day and night, saying...
En 40:1 ...I saw thousands of thousands and ten thousand times ten thousand —I saw a multitude beyond number and reckoning who stood before the Lord of hosts.	**Rev 5:11 ISV** Then I looked, and I heard the voices of many angels... surrounding the throne. They numbered 10,000's times 10,000 and thousands times thousands.
En 40:2 On the four sides of the Lord of hosts I saw four presences...	**Rev 4:6** ...on each side of the throne, are four living creatures...

Book of Enoch	*New Testament*
En 45:3 On that day, My Chosen One will sit on the throne of glory, *He* will test their works, and they will have *many* places of rest beyond number.	**Matt 25:31-32** ...then he will sit on his glorious throne. [32] Before him will be gathered all the nations, and he will separate people one from another... **John 14:2** In my Father's house are many rooms.
En 45:4-5 Then I will send My Chosen One to live among them. I will transform heaven and make it an eternal blessing and *eternal* light; [5] I will transform the earth and make it a blessing, and I will cause My chosen to live there...	**Rev 7:15 WEB** He who sits on the throne will spread his tabernacle over them. **2Pe 3:13** But according to his promise we are waiting for new heavens and a new earth in which righteousness dwells.
En 46:3 This is the Son of Man... He reveals the treasures of the hidden things...	**Col 2:2-3** ...Christ, [3] in whom are hidden all the treasures of wisdom and knowledge.
En 48:1 In that place, I saw the fountain of righteousness that was inexhaustible. Around it were many fountains of wisdom. All the thirsty drank of them and were filled with wisdom. Their dwellings were with the righteous, holy, and elect.	**John 4:14** ...but whoever drinks of the water that I will give him will never be thirsty again. The water that I will give him will become in him a spring of water welling up to eternal life. **Rev 21:6** To the thirsty I will give from the spring of the water of life without payment.

Book of Enoch	New Testament
En 48:7 For He has preserved the inheritance of the righteous, because they have hated and despised this world of unrighteousness, and have hated all its works and ways in the name of the Lord of hosts.	**Gal 1:4** ...who gave himself for our sins to deliver us from the present evil age, according to the will of our God and Father... **1John 2:15** Do not love the world or the things in the world.
En 48:9 ...so will they burn in the presence of the holy. ...they will sink in the presence of the righteous.	**Rev 14:10** ...will be tormented with fire and sulfur in the presence of the holy angels and in the presence of the Lamb.
En 48:10 ...they denied the Lord of hosts and His Anointed.	**Jude 1:4 KJV** ...denying the only Lord God, and our Lord Jesus Christ.
En 51:2 ...for the day of their salvation is near.	**Luke 21:28** ...your redemption is drawing near.
En 54:6 ...leading astray those who dwell on the earth.	**Rev 13:14** ...deceives those who dwell on earth...
En 58:5 ...it has become bright as the sun upon earth, and the darkness is past.	**1John 2:8** ...because the darkness is passing away and the true light is already shining.
En 61:10 ...all the angels of power...	**2Th 1:7 ASV** ...the angels of his power...

Book of Enoch	*New Testament*
En 62:2,4-5 ² The word of His mouth slays all the sinners, and all the unrighteous are destroyed at His presence. ...⁴ Then pain will come over them like a woman in child birth whose labor is severe, when her child enters the mouth of the womb, and she has pain in giving birth. ⁵ One group of them will look to the other, and they will be terrified. Their faces will be dismayed, and pain will seize them when they see that Son of Man sitting on the throne of His glory.	**2 Thes 2:8** ...the Lord Jesus will kill with the breath of his mouth... **1 Thes 5:3** ...then sudden destruction will come upon them as labor pains come upon a pregnant woman, and they will not escape. **Matt 25:31** When the Son of man shall come in his glory, then shall he sit upon the throne of his glory.
En 62:3,5 ³ ...the kings, the mighty, the exalted... ⁵ ...they will be terrified... and pain will seize them when they see that Son of Man sitting on the throne of His glory.	**Rev 6:15-16** Then the kings of the earth and the great ones... ¹⁶ calling to the mountains and rocks, "Fall on us and hide us from the face of him who is seated on the throne, and from the wrath of the Lamb...
En 62:14 They will eat with the Son of Man, lie down, and rise up forever and ever.	**Rev 3:20** If anyone hears my voice and opens the door, I will come in to him and eat with him, and he with me.

Book of Enoch	New Testament
En 63:8 MSV His judgments show no partiality. Or **En 63:8** His judgments have no respect of persons. (Charles)	**Rom 2:11 ESV** For God shows no partiality. Or **Rom 2:11 KJV** For there is no respect of persons with God.
En 65:4 ...a voice spoke from heaven...	**Matt 3:17** ...and behold, a voice from heaven said...
En 67:5-7 ...in that valley... ⁶ it produced a smell of sulfur, mixed it with the waters; and the valley of the angels who led astray *mankind* burned beneath the land. ⁷ Through the valleys of that land run rivers of fire, where these angels are punished who corrupted those who live on the earth.	**Matt 13:42** ...throw them into the fiery furnace. **Matt 25:41** Depart from me, you cursed, into the eternal fire prepared for the devil and his angels. **Rev 20:10** ...and the devil who had deceived them was thrown into the lake of fire and sulfur...
En 69:22 ...the spirits... of the winds...	**Rev 7:1 ASV** ...four angels... holding the four winds of the earth...
En 86:1 ...and behold, a star fell from heaven!	**Rev 9:1** ...and I saw a star fallen from heaven to earth...
En 91:4 *(The righteous)* will walk in eternal light...	**1John 1:7** ...we walk in the light...

Book of Enoch	*New Testament*
En 93:15 The first heaven will depart and pass away; a new heaven will appear...	**Rev 21:1** ...I saw a new heaven and a new earth: for the first heaven and the first earth have passed away...
En 94:8 Woe to you, those who are rich, for you have trusted in your riches.	**Luke 6:24** ...woe to you who are rich, for you have received your consolation.
En 97:8-10 Woe to you who acquire silver and gold in unrighteousness and say, 'We have become wealthy with riches, have possessions, and have gained everything that we wanted. Now let us do what we planned, for we have gathered silver, and we have many workmen in our houses. Our granaries are full to the brim'... For your riches will not remain... and you will be given over to a great curse	**Luke 12:19-20** *(Compare the parable of the rich man whose barns were full, and who said to himself,)* "Soul, you have ample goods laid up for many years; relax, eat, drink, be merry." But God said to him, 'Fool! This night your soul is required of you, and the things you have prepared, whose will they be?'
En 100:3 The horse will walk breast deep in the blood of sinners	**Rev 14:20** blood flowed from the winepress, as high as a horse's bridle

Book of Enoch	*New Testament*
En 104:10 Now I know this mystery, that sinners will alter and pervert the words of righteousness in many ways, and will speak wicked words, and lie, and practice great deception	**1Ti 4:1-2** the Spirit expressly says that in later times some will depart from the faith. . . through the insincerity of liars
En 108:8 who love God and loved neither gold nor silver nor any of the good things that are in the world	**1John 2:15** Do not love the world or the things in the world.
En 108:11 the generation of light	**Luke 16:8** the sons of light **John 12:36** become sons of light
En 108:12 I will seat each on the throne of his honor.	**Matt 19:28 WEB** you also will sit on twelve thrones **Rev 3:21** The one who conquers, I will grant him to sit with me on my throne

COMMENTARY

These are excerpts of commentary from the versions released by the translators of the Book of Enoch. They have been abridged and edited to fit the format and presentation of the MSV. Full, original commentaries can be found in the public domain.

The translators agreed that multiple authors wrote the Book of Enoch. This leads us to wonder if the material is genuine. Was Enoch himself even involved with these texts? The simple facts are as follows: Anything Enoch wrote would have been in a language that predated the Tower of Babel and thus would have required translation and alteration to be understood by later generations. The texts of the Book of Enoch date from around 400-200 BC, but that does not mean their origins started there. Enoch was taken by God near 3000 BC, or about 5000 years ago. Any works so old would likely be translations of translations of translations, etc. It is only logical for multiple authors to have altered and updated this work over such a long period, often including "modern" phrases, names, and people groups from their era.

For example, a new translation of the Holy Bible with phrases, country names, and sentence structure from the modern era does not mean the scriptures originated in modern times. It only means that particular version was written down in modern times. The oldest parts of the Book of Enoch would have been 1500 years old when Moses wrote Genesis, and Enoch would likely be the only existing work to survive a simultaneous, planetary-wide language shift.

With this in mind, we must turn to the Holy Bible to tell us if we can value the Book of Enoch as genuine. Nearly every writer of the New Testament has clear influence from the Book of Enoch in their writings. This obvious interconnection between scripture and the Book of Enoch culminates in Revelation, where portions of the biblical book are a retelling of the visions and writings from the Book of Enoch.

SHOULD THE BOOK OF ENOCH
BE INCLUDED IN THE BIBLE?

One of the most asked questions regarding the Book of Enoch is whether or not this work should be canonized as part of the Holy Bible. The short answer is no.

Enoch 37:7 states, "It would be better to declare *only* to the men of ancient times, but even for those that come after we will not withhold the beginning of wisdom." In other words, the people who lived before Noah's flood were the primary target audience for this work. Much of the text focuses on assuring the reader that yes, God is aware of the sins of the fallen angels, and yes, they will be punished for their sins.

The end times prophecies of Enoch were then carried on by the Apostles through divine revalation in the form of the Holy Bible. The text states, "but even for those that come after we will not withhold the beginning of wisdom." The Book of Enoch is worthy of study and brings many benefits; thus, it has been preserved and is available for our use. But it cannot compare to the Holy Bible in that every word of the Bible applies to life in any era.

Another problem with canonizing the Book of Enoch is that the text has been altered over thousands of years. Many ancient scribes and translators tried to fix missing or broken passages. Some added their own passages. One famous example is Enoch 71:13, where a scribe was confused by a missing passage and then altered other verses to say that Enoch himself was the Messiah instead of Jesus. While we can reconstruct and repair this damage, we don't know the exact form of the original text. For something to be included in the Bible, we must have full confidence that it is the inerrant Word of God, and the Book of Enoch cannot hold up to that level of scrutiny.

Still, the use of the Book of Enoch in influencing much of the New Testament gives us confidence to trust and value this work. Its content, tenor, and intent line up beautifully with the work of the Holy Bible.

GEORGE H. SCHODDE

(Enoch) is of importance and interest for us, not only on account of the mysterious prominence given him in Gen 5, but especially from the fact that an inspired writer of the New Testament, Jude, in his letter verse 14, mentions him as a prophet, and produces a quotation from a book attributed to the patriarch. The existence of such a book does not, however, rest on the authority of this statement alone; but in the early literature of the church, there is a whole chain of evidences to this effect. Nearly all of the church Fathers knew of an apocryphal Book of Enoch, and their description of the work and citations from it prove satisfactorily that it was virtually the same as that which now lies before us.

R. H. CHARLES

Nearly all the writers of the New Testament were familiar with it (the Book of Enoch), and were more or less influenced by it in thought and diction. It is quoted as a genuine production of Enoch by St. Jude, and as Scripture by St. Barnabas. The authors of the Book of Jubilees, the Apocalypse of Barucb, and 4 Ezra, laid it under contribution. With the earlier Fathers and Apologists it had all the weight of a canonical book.

Written by W. O. E. Osterley in the R. H. Charles version:

As the Book of Enoch is, in some respects, the most notable extant apocalyptic work outside the canonical Scriptures, it will not be inappropriate to offer a few remarks here on the Apocalyptic Literature generally. In writing about the books which belong to this literature, Prof. Burkitt says very pointedly that "they are the most characteristic survival of what I will venture to call, with all its narrowness and its incoherence, the heroic age of Jewish history, the age when the nation attempted to realize in action the part of the peculiar people of God. It ended in catastrophe, but the nation left two successors, the Christian Church and the Rabbinical Schools, each of which carried on some of the old national aims. And of the two it was the Christian Church that was most faithful to the ideas enshrined in the Apocalypses, and it did consider itself, not without some reason, the fulfilment of those ideas. What is wanted, therefore, in studying the Apocalypses is, above all, sympathy with the ideas that underlie them, and especially with the belief in the New Age. And those who believe that in Christianity a new Era really did dawn for us ought, I think, to have that sympathy. . . . We study the Apocalypses to learn how our spiritual ancestors hoped again that God would make all right in the end; and that we, their children, are here to-day studying them is an indication that their hope was not wholly unfounded."

Hope is, indeed, the main underlying motive—power which prompted the writers of the Apocalypses. And this hope is the more intensive and ardent in that it shines forth from a background which is dark with despair; for the Apocalyptists despaired of the world in which they lived, a world in which the godly were of no account, while the wicked seemed too often triumphant and prosperous. With evil everywhere around, the Apocalyptists saw no hope for the world as it was; for such a world there was no remedy, only destruction; if the good were ever to triumph it must be in a new world. Despairing, therefore, of the world around them, the Apocalyptists centered their hope upon a world to come, where the righteous would come to their own and evil would find no place. It is this thought which underlies the opening words of the Book of Enoch: "The words of the blessing of Enoch, wherewith he blessed the elect and righteous, who will be living in the day of tribulation, when all the wicked and godless are to be removed." Nowhere in this book is the essence of this hope more beautifully expressed than in a short metrical piece in the first chapter:

"But with the righteous, He will make peace.

He will protect the chosen,
    and mercy will be on them.
They will all belong to God,
    they will prosper,
    and they will all be blessed.
He will help them all,
    light will appear to them,
    and He will make peace with them."
                (Enoch 1:8)

Now, since, as we have seen, the Apocalyptists despair of any bettering of the present world, and therefore contemplate its destruction as the preliminary of the new order of things, they look away from this world in their visions of the future; they conceive of other-worldly forces coming into play in the reconstitution of things, and of society generally; and since these are other-worldly forces the supernatural plays a great part in the Apocalyptic Literature. This supernatural coloring will often strike the reader of this literature as fantastic, and at times bizarre; but this should not be permitted to obscure the reality which often lies behind these weird shadows. Mental visions are not always easily expressed in words; the seer who in a vision has received a message in some fantastic guise necessarily has the impression upon his mind of what he has seen when giving his message; and when he describes his vision the picture he presents is, in the nature of the case, more fantastic to the ear of the hearer than to the eye of him who saw it. Allowance should be made for this; especially by us Westerners who are so lacking in the rich imaginativeness of the Easterner. Our love of literalness hinders the play of the imagination because we are so apt to "materialize" a mental picture presented by another. The Apocalypses were written by and for Easterners, and we cannot do justice to them unless we remember this; but it would be best if we could get into the Easterner mind and look at things from that point of view.

The Importance of the Book of Enoch for the Study of Christian Origins

This is a subject which cannot be thoroughly appreciated without studying the book in detail, especially from its doctrinal standpoint, and seeing in how many aspects it represents the doctrine and the popular conceptions of the Jews during the two last pre-Christian centuries. To do this here would involve a far too extended investigation; it must suffice to indicate a few of the many points which should be studied; from these it will be seen how important the book is for the study of Christian origins. Charles says that "the influence of Enoch on the New Testament has been greater than that of all the other apocryphal and pseudepigraphical books put together"; and he gives a formidable list of passages in the New Testament which "either in phraseology or idea directly depend on, or are illustrative of, passages in Enoch," as well as a further list showing that various doctrines in Enoch had "an undoubted share in molding the corresponding New Testament doctrines." These passages should be studied—and they will be found to be a most interesting study. Another book of great value and interest—also already quoted—is Burkitt's Jewish and Christian Apocalypses. In dealing with the subject of Enoch and the Gospels, this writer points out that the former "contains a serious attempt to account for the presence of Evil in human history, and this attempt claims our attention, because it is in essentials the view presupposed in the Gospels, especially in the Synoptic Gospels. It is when you study Matthew, Mark, and Luke against the background of the Books of Enoch that you see them in their true perspective. In saying this I have no intention of detracting from the importance of what the Gospels report to us. On the contrary, it puts familiar words into their proper setting. Indeed, it seems to me that some of the best-known sayings of Jesus only appear in their true light if regarded as Midrash upon words and concepts that were familiar to those who heard the Prophet of Galilee, though now they have been forgotten by Jew and Christian alike" (p. 21). He then gives an illustration of this from Mat 12:43-45, Luk 11:24-26. Of still greater interest are his remarks upon the relationship between Enoch 62 and Mat 25:31-46; he believes that "the Similitudes of Enoch are presupposed in the scene from Matthew." The whole of the discussion which follows should be read.

The special points of interest that should be studied in seeking to realize the importance of these books of Enoch for the study of Christian origins are the problems of evil, including, of course, the subjects of demonology, and future judgment; the Messiah and the Messianic Kingdom—the title "Son of Man" is of special importance--and the Resurrection. There are, of course, other subjects which will suggest themselves in studying the book.

RICHARD LAURENCE

(The author of *The Evolution of Christianity* wrote this commentary anonymously for the Richard Laurence translation.)

On Chapters and Verses:
Author's note: Richard Laurence did not always use the chapter and verse numbering that later translators used, such as R. H. Charles. His chapters remain within 1 chapter of the numbers found in the MSV.

In the Authorized Version of the Epistle of Jude, we read the following words:

"Enoch also, the seventh from Adam, prophesied of these, saying, Behold, the Lord cometh with ten thousands of his saints, to execute judgment upon all, and to convince all that are ungodly among them of all their ungodly deeds which they have ungodly committed, and of all their hard speeches which ungodly sinners have spoken against Him."

Modern research sees in the Epistle of Jude a work of the second century: but as orthodox theologians accept its contents as the inspired utterance of an Apostle, let us diligently search the Hebrew Scriptures for this important forecast of the second Advent of the Messiah. In vain we turn over the pages of the sacred Canon; not even in the Apocrypha can we trace one line from the pen of the marvelous being to whom uninterrupted immortality is assigned by apostolic interpretation of Genesis 5:24. Were the prophecies of Enoch, therefore, accepted as a Divine revelation on that momentous day when Jesus explained the Scriptures, after his resurrection, to Jude and his apostolic brethren; and have we moderns betrayed our trust by excluding an inspired record from the Bible?

Reverting to the second century of Christianity, we find Irenaeus and Clement of Alexandria citing the Book of Enoch without questioning its sacred character. Thus, Irenaeus, assigning to the Book of Enoch an authenticity analogous to that of Mosaic literature, affirms that Enoch, although a man, filled the office of God's messenger to the angels. Tertullian, who flourished at the close of the first and at the beginning of the second century, whilst admitting that the "Scripture of Enoch" is not received by some because it is not included in the Hebrew Canon, speaks of the author as "the most ancient prophet, Enoch," and of the book as the divinely inspired autograph of that immortal patriarch, preserved by Noah in the ark, or miraculously reproduced by him through the inspiration of the Holy Spirit. Tertullian adds, "But as Enoch has spoken in the same scripture of the Lord, and 'every scripture suitable for edification is divinely inspired,' let us reject nothing which belongs to us. It may now seem to have been disavowed by the Jews like all other scripture which speaks of Christ—a fact which should cause us no surprise, as they were not to receive him, even when personally addressed by himself." These views Tertullian confirms by appealing to the testimony of the Apostle Jude. The Book of Enoch was therefore as sacred as the Psalms or Isaiah in the eyes of the famous theologian, on whom modern orthodoxy relies as the chief canonist of New Testament scripture.

Origen (A.D. 254), in quoting Hebrew literature, assigns to the Book of Enoch the same authority as to the Psalms. In polemical discussion with Celsus, he affirms that the work of the antediluvian patriarch was not accepted in the Churches as Divine; and modern theologians have accordingly assumed that he rejected its inspiration: but the extent to which he adopts its language and ideas discloses personal conviction that Enoch was one of the greatest of the prophets. Thus, in his treatise on the angels, we read: "We are not to suppose that a special office has been assigned by mere accident to a particular angel: as to Raphael, the work of curing and healing; to Gabriel, the direction of wars; to Michael, the duty of hearing the prayers and supplications of men." From what source but assumed revelation could

Origen obtain and publish these circumstantial details of ministerial administration in heaven?

Turning to the Book of Enoch we read: "After this I besought the angel of peace, who proceeded with me, to explain all that was concealed. I said to him, Who are those whom I have seen on the four sides, and whose words I have heard and written down. He replied. The first is the merciful, the patient, the holy Michael. The second is he who presides over every suffering and every affliction of the sons of men, the holy Raphael. The third, who presides over all that is powerful, is Gabriel. And the fourth, who presides over repentance and the hope of those who will inherit eternal life, is Phanuel." We thus discover the source of Origen's apparently superhuman knowledge, and detect his implicit trust in the Book of Enoch as a Divine revelation.

When primitive Christianity had freely appropriated the visions of Enoch as the materials of constructive dogmas, this remarkable book gradually sank into oblivion, disappeared out of Western Christendom, and was eventually forgotten by a Church, which unconsciously perpetuated its teaching as the miraculous revelations of Christianity.

The Book of Enoch, unknown to Europe for nearly a thousand years, except through the fragments preserved by Georgius Syncellus (circa 792, A.D.), was at length discovered by Bruce in Abyssinia, who brought home three copies of the Ethiopic version in 1773, respecting which he writes: "Amongst the articles I consigned to the library at Paris was a very beautiful and magnificent copy of the Prophecies of Enoch, in large quarto; another , is amongst the Books of Scripture which I brought home, standing immediately before the Book of Job, which is its proper place in the Abyssinian Canon; and a third copy I have presented to the, Bodleian Library at Oxford, by the hands of Br. Douglas, the Bishop of Carlisle."

This priceless manuscript, destined, some day, to reveal the forgotten source of many Christian dogmas and mysteries, rested in Bodleian obscurity, until presented to the world through an English translation by Dr. Laurence, Archbishop of Cashel, formerly Professor of Hebrew at Oxford, who issued his first edition in 1821, in apparent unconsciousness that he was giving to mankind the theological fossils through which we, in the clearer light of our generation, may study the "Evolution of Christianity."

The scarcity of Archbishop Laurence's translation, before the publication of the second edition in 1833, produced an impression in Germany that the work had been suppressed by its author; but this report is contradicted in the preface to the third edition, issued in 1838, in response to a large order from America.

The Book of Enoch excited more interest on the Continent than in England. It was translated into German by Dr. Hoffman in 1838, into Latin by Grfrorer in 1840, again into German by Dillmann in 1853, and has been discussed by Weisse, Lucke, Hilgenfeld, and Kalisch, the latter of whom uttered the prediction, that the Book of Enoch "will one day be employed as a most important witness in the history of religious dogmas." The day and the hour have come, the clock has struck, and in thus publishing an edition of Archbishop Laurence's translation of the Book of Enoch, we place within the reach of all readers of the English language, the means of studying the pre-Christian origin of Christian mysteries.

Ignorance of the contents of the Apocrypha, as canonized by the Church of Rome, is so general in England that many otherwise well-informed people imagine that the Book of Enoch may be found in its pages, whereas it has been lost to all English readers, except those who may possess or have access to copies of the English translation last issued in 1838. On this aspect of the question Archbishop Laurence writes:—

"The fate of the Apocryphal writings in general has been singular. On one side, from the influence of theological opinion or theological caprice, they have been sometimes injudiciously admitted into the Canon of Scripture; while on the other side, from an over-anxiety to preserve that Canon inviolate, they have been not simply rejected, but loaded with every epithet of contempt and obloquy. The feelings perhaps of both parties have on such occasions run away with their judgment. For writings of this description, whatever may or may not be their claim to inspiration, are at least of considerable utility, where they indicate the theological opinions of the periods at which they were composed. This I apprehend to be peculiarly the case of the Book of Enoch; which, as having been manifestly written before the doctrines of Christianity were promulgated to the world, must afford us, when it refers to the nature and character of the Messiah, as it repeatedly does so refer, credible proof of what were the Jewish opinions upon those points before the birth of Christ; and consequently before the possible predominance of the Christian creed."

Archbishop Laurence thus clearly recognized that the visions of Enoch preceded the teaching of Jesus; but it was not given to him, or to his generation, to see how deeply his conclusions affected the supernatural claims of Christianity.

Turning to the contents of the Book of Enoch, the first six chapters announce the condemnation of transgressors and the blessings of the righteous, through the triumphal advent of the Messiah, forecast in the famous prediction quoted by the author of the Epistle attributed to Jude.

Chapters 7 to 16 record the descent of two hundred angels on the earth, their selection of wives, the birth of their gigantic offspring, and the instruction of mankind in the manufacture of offensive and defensive weapons, the fabrication of mirrors, the workmanship of jewelry, and the use of cosmetics and dyes, combined with lessons in sorcery, astrology, divination, and astronomy.

The advent of the angels multiplies transgressions on earth; they are condemned to "the lowest depths of the fire in torments," and Enoch, as the messenger of God, announces to them the eternity of their punishment.

Chapters 17 to 36 give a graphic description of the miraculous journeys of Enoch in the company of an angel, from whom he learns the secrets of creation and the mysteries of Infinity. From the top of a lofty mountain "which reached to heaven," he beheld the receptacles of light, thunder, and lightning, "the great darkness or mountains of gloom which constitute winter, the mouths of rivers and of the deep, the stone which supports the corners of the earth, and the four winds which bear up the earth, and constitute the pillars of heaven."

But had not the Book of Enoch disappeared for centuries out of Europe, before the persecution of Galileo and the martyrdom of Bruno? We answer that its teaching had survived, as numerous other superstitions have passed from generation to generation long after all knowledge of their origin has been lost to the theologians who accept them as Divine.

In the "Evolution of Christianity" we cite the following passage from Irenaeus: "It is impossible that the Gospels can be more or less than they are. For as there are four zones in the world which we inhabit, and four principal winds, while the Church is spread abroad throughout the earth, and the pillar and basis of the Church is the gospel and the spirit of life, it is right that she should have four pillars exhaling immortality on every side, and bestowing renewed vitality on men. From which fact it follows that the Word has given us four versions of the Gospel, united by one spirit." We now recognize that this fanciful theory of a limited number of Evangelists is based on the cosmology of Enoch; and if in the second century, Irenaeus accepted the visions of an antediluvian patriarch as facts, the traditional survival of the earth's "corner stone" doubtless controlled the orthodox astronomy of mediaeval theologians.

Proceeding on his journey with the angel Uriel, Enoch furthermore beheld the prison of the fallen angels, in which struggling columns of fire ascended from an appalling abyss. He saw the place which the spirits of the dead await the day of judgment; he looked upon the trees of knowledge and of life, exhaling fragrant odors from leaves which never withered, and from fruit which ever bloomed and he beheld the "great and glorious wonder" of the celestial stars, coming forth through the "gates of heaven."

Chapters 37 to 71 record the second vision of wisdom, divided into three parables. The first depicts the future happiness and glory of the elect, whom Enoch beheld reclining on couches in the habitations of angels, or standing in thousands of thousands and myriads of myriads before the throne of God, blessing and glorifying Him with celestial song, as the Holy, Holy Lord of spirits, before whom righteousness eternally dwells.

As Enoch uttered his prophecies respecting the elect, before the existence of Christianity, it is important to learn in what sense he understood the doctrine of election. The language of the first parable happily leaves no room for doubt—"The righteous will be elected for their good works duly weighed by the Lord of Spirits." Election, therefore, traced to its original source, means nothing more than Divine "selection of the fittest"—a theory more consistent with the justice of God, than the capricious choice of the metamorphical potter, whose arbitrary fashioning of plastic clay symbolized, in Pauline theology, the doctrine of predestination.

The second parable (45-55) demands the absorbed attention of modern Jews and Gentiles for it is either the inspired forecast of a great Hebrew prophet, predicting with miraculous accuracy the future teaching of Jesus of Nazareth, or the Semitic romance from which the latter borrowed His conceptions of the triumphant return of the Son of man, to occupy a judicial throne in the midst of rejoicing saints and trembling sinners, expectant of everlasting happiness or eternal fire and whether these celestial visions be accepted as human or Divine, they have exercised so vast an influence on the destinies of mankind for nearly two thousand years, that candid and impartial seekers after religious truth can no longer delay inquiry into the relationship of the Book of Enoch with the revelation, or the evolution, of Christianity.

The third parable (56-70) recurs, with glowing eloquence, to the inexhaustible theme of Messianic glory, and again depicts the happy future of the righteous in contrast with the appalling misery of the wicked. It also records the supernatural control of the elements, through the action of individual angels presiding over the winds, the sea, hail, frost, dew, the lightning's flash, and reverberating thunder.

Chapters 71 to 81 contain the "book of the revolutions of the luminaries of heaven," the sun, the moon, and the stars, controlled in their movements by the administration of angels. In commenting on this section of the Book of Enoch, Archbishop Laurence says, "This system of astronomy is precisely that of an untutored, but accurate observer of the heavens. He describes the eastern and western parts of heaven, where the sun and moon rise and set, as divided each into six different gates, through which those orbs of light pass at their respective periods. In the denomination of these gates he begins with that through which the sun passes at the winter solstice; and this he terms the first gate. It of course answers to the sign of Capricornus; and is the southernmost point to which the sun reaches, both at rising and setting. The next gate, at which the sun arrives in its progress towards the east at rising, and towards the west at setting, and which answers to the sign of Aquarius, he terms the second gate. The next, in continuation of the same course of the sun, which answers to the sign of Pisces, he terms the third gate. The fourth gate in his description is that which is situated due east at sunrising, and due west at sun-setting, and which, answering to the sign of Aries, the sun enters at the vernal equinox. With this fourth gate he commences his account of the sun's annual circuit, and of the consequent change in the length of day and night at the various seasons of the year. His fifth gate is now to be found in the sun's progress northwards, and answers to the sign of Taurus. And his sixth gate is situated still further north; which, answering to the sign of Gemini, concludes at the most northern point of heaven to which the sun arrives, and from which it turns at the summer solstice, again to measure back its course southwards.

"Hence it happens, that the same gates which answers to the six signs alluded to in the sun's passage from the winter to the summer solstice, necessarily also answer to the remaining six of the twelve signs of the Zodiac in its passage back again.

"The turning of the sun both at the winter and summer solstices, the first at the most southern, the last at the most northern point of its progress, must have always struck the eye of those who contemplated the variety as well as the splendor of its daily appearance. The astronomy of the apocryphal Enoch was perhaps formed in this respect upon the same principles as the astronomy of Homer."

Chapters 83 to 89 contain a vision of Enoch giving an allegorical forecast of the history of the world up to the kingdom of the Messiah.

Chapter 92 records a series of prophecies extending from Enoch's own time to about one thousand years beyond the present generation. In the system of chronology adopted, a day stands for hundred, and a week for seven hundred years. Reference is made to the deluge, the call of Abraham, the Mosaic dispensation, the building and the destruction of the Temple of Solomon. If, however, the Book of Enoch had reached us through the Western, as well as the Ethiopic Canon, apologetic theologians would doubtless affirm that centuries are but trifles in prophetic time; and that the predictions of the great antediluvian prophet shall, sooner or later, attain miraculous fulfilment.

Chapters 93 to 104 contain the eloquent exhortations of Enoch, addressed to his children, in which he anticipates Jesus in pronouncing the doom of sinners and the joys of saints, and gives utterance to the most emphatic assurance of immortality which has ever flowed from human lips: "Fear not, ye souls of the righteous, but wait with patient hope for the day of your death in righteousness. Grieve not because your souls descend in trouble and sorrow to the receptacle of the dead;

for great joy shall be yours, like that of the angels in heaven. And when you die, sinners say concerning you, 'As we die the righteous die. What profit have they in their works? Behold, like us, they expire in sorrow and in darkness. What advantage have they over us? Henceforward are we equal; for behold they are dead, and never will they again perceive the light.' But now I swear to you, ye righteous ... that I comprehend this mystery; that I have read the tablet of heaven, have seen the writing of the holy ones, and have discovered what is written and impressed on it concerning you. I have seen that all goodness, joy, and glory have been prepared for you. . . . The spirits of you who die in righteousness shall exist and rejoice; and their remembrance shall be before the face of the Mighty One from generation to generation." How profound the impression necessarily produced on the Semitic imagination by this impassioned language, uttered in an age of faith in inspired dreams and celestial visions by a supposed visitant of the unseen world, who had conversed with angels in the presence of the Lord of spirits!

The final chapter of the Book of Enoch records the birth of Noah, and the further prophecies of Enoch, addressed to Methuselah on the subject of the birth of Noah and the future deluge.

The Book of Enoch (establishes) its complete identity with the parallel passage in the Epistle of Jude —an identity of marvelous clearness when we consider that the original version reaches us through translations and retranslations from Aramaean, Greek, and Ethiopic, and now assumes the modern form of Anglo-Saxon. Archbishop Laurence, although convinced that the apostle cited the Greek version of the extant Ethiopic manuscripts, was not aware that the last sentence of his quotation is present in the text. We have discovered it in chapter 27:2 of the Book of Enoch (MSV); and in thus perfecting the parallelism between prophet and apostle, have placed beyond controversy that, in the eyes of the author of an Epistle accepted as Divine revelation, the Book of Enoch was the inspired production of an antediluvian patriarch.

The attention of theologians has been concentrated on the passage in the Epistle of Jude because the author specifically names the prophet; but the cumulative coincidence of language and ideas in Enoch and the authors of New Testament Scripture, as disclosed in the parallel passages which we have collated, clearly indicates that the work of the Semitic Milton was the inexhaustible source from which Evangelists and Apostles, borrowed their conceptions of the resurrection, judgment, immortality, perdition, and of the universal reign of righteousness under the eternal dominion of the Son of man. This culminates in the Revelation of John, which adapts the visions of Enoch to Christianity with modifications in which we miss the sublime simplicity of the great master of apocalyptic prediction, who prophesied in the name of the antediluvian patriarch.

It is important to observe that it was not the practice of early Christian writers to name the authors whose language and ideas they borrowed. When we therefore detect the teaching and diction of Enoch in Gospels and Epistles, our conclusions are analogous to those of the orthodox theologians who identify passages of Scripture in the pages of the ante-Nicene Fathers, although frequently cited from unnamed sources, with an obscurity of expression more dubious in attestation of their origin, than the remarkable clearness with which the language of Enoch may be recognized in the New Testament. Biblical analysts may question obscure traces of evangelical diction in apostolic Fathers; but what candid and impartial inquirer can doubt the Enochian origin of the "Son of man sitting upon the throne of his glory"—the "new heaven" and the "new earth;" the "many habitations" of the elect, and "the everlasting fire prepared for the devil and his angels"?

We have merely collated some of the most striking instances of parallel passages in the Book of Enoch and in the New Testament. Our readers can supplement our labors through their own research, in further attestation of the controlling influence exercised by the uncanonical author on the language and ideas of canonical works.

Some orthodox theologians, unwilling to admit that an apostle quoted an apocryphal book, contend that Jude referred to a traditional utterance of the ancient patriarch; but this obviously fanciful theory inevitably vanishes in the presence of the numerous passages from the Book of Enoch, which enter into the composition of New Testament Scripture. Other pious apologists affirm the post-Christian authorship of the book, a theory which involves the most improbable assumption that an author, familiar with the story of a suffering and crucified Messiah, uttered fictitious predictions in the name of an ancient prophet, which depicted the career of the Son of man on earth as the triumphal march of a victorious king. Again, theologians who shrink from the admission that the language and ideas of evangelists and apostles were anticipated in an apocryphal book, suggest that the Messianic passages contain Christian interpolations. But if modern defenders of the faith thus accuse primitive saints and martyrs of literary forgery, how can they accept an infallible Jew Testament at the hands of men thus guilty of conspiring for the deception of posterity? Convinced of the honesty of early Christians, we concur with the opinion of Archbishop Laurence, confirmed by Hoffman, that the passages in question are so intimately interwoven with the general context that they cannot be removed without evidently destroying the texture of the whole.

It cannot be said that internal evidence attests the superiority of the Old Testament to the Book of Enoch; for no Hebrew prophet is more eloquent than its author in denouncing iniquity, commending righteousness, and inviting all men to place implicit trust in the final vindication of Divine justice.

Christianity obviously borrows the terrors of eternal fire from the Book of Enoch. Evangelists and Apostles define the duration of Divine retribution by aeons of aeons, or millions of millions of years, expressive of eternity. It is true that the word aeon can be used in the sense of finite time, but when the authors of New Testament Scripture speak of aeonian fire they obviously mean eternal flames. Modern humanity, shrinking from so merciless a view of Divine retribution, suggests that when sinners have been tortured for aeons of aeons they may look forward hopefully to the future. It is questionable whether final despair would not be preferable to this form of "hope deferred;" but if modern believers adopt the terminable theory of aeonian fire, this commutation of sentence becomes equally applicable to the devil and his angels, whose punishment has been decreed of same duration as that of human sinners; and thus the traditional enemies of God and man may hope for joyful restoration to fellowship with Gabriel, Michael, and Raphael, and communion with the saints, whom they once sought to betray by arts infernal. And as the righteous are also only promised their rewards in heaven for aeons of aeons, if these words mean not eternity, saints may fear, whilst sinners hope for, the vicissitudes of aeonian futurity. Again, as the dominion of the Messiah, and even the power of God, are depicted of aeonian duration, any limitation of the infinite in the sacred terminology—aeons of aeons— imperils the eternal in Divinity.

Theologians who seek to vindicate Divine clemency through the dubious expedient of substituting aeonian for eternal retribution, overlook the fact that their theory imputes to Divine wisdom the adoption of torture as the most effectual means of transforming sinners into saints,—a theory which practically invites us to follow the Divine example by torturing our criminals into reformation.

The Book of Enoch teaches the pre-existence-of the Son of Man, the Elect One, the Messiah, who "from the beginning existed in secret," -and whose "name was invoked in the presence of the Lord of spirits, before the sun and the signs were created." The author also refers to the "other Power who was upon earth over the water on that day,"—an apparent reference to the language of Gen 1:2. We have thus the Lord of spirits, the Elect One, and a third Power, seemingly foreshadowing the Trinity of futurity; but although Enoch's ideal Messiah doubtless exercised an important influence on primitive conceptions of the

Divinity of the Son of man, we fail to identify his obscure reference to another "Power" with the Trinitarianism of the Alexandrine school; more especially as "angels of power" abound in the visions of Enoch.

That remarkable passage in the Book of Enoch, which declares that the heathen "sacrificed to devils as to gods," is the obvious source of that superstition through which primitive Christianity saw in Olympian deities, not the mere phantoms of man's imagination, but the fallen angels who, driven forth from heaven, sought compensation in spiritual dominion on earth,—a superstition still further confirmed by universal belief in miracles, wrought, not merely by the Supreme, but by subordinate powers, whether good or evil.

Archbishop Laurence, when Professor of Hebrew in the University of Oxford, translated the Book of Enoch within the walls of the Bodleian Library, and when appealed to by the Rev. I. M. Butt, in 1827, to publish, the Ethiopic original, answered, "I cannot, the manuscript not being my own, but belonging to the University of Oxford." In his preface to the third edition of his translation, the Archbishop adds, "If the University of Oxford would oblige the literary world by publishing the original Ethiopic from the manuscript in its possession, I am persuaded that Ethiopic scholars would not be wanting to accomplish more than has been hitherto done for this long regretted book, after its sleep of ages." Since these words were written, great progress has been made in the study of comparative philology; and there are now doubtless many eminent linguists who could still further illumine the pages of the Book of Enoch, through co-operative criticism of the Ethiopic text. Is not the time therefore come for the University of Oxford to publish the original manuscript in their possession, that learned Jews and Gentiles may study the inspired predictions of a great Hebrew prophet, or admire the sublime imagery of the Semitic Milton who ascended to the heavens to dramatize Divinity?

Archbishop Laurence's translation, now however, places the Book of Enoch within the reach of all English readers. Catholics may disregard its contents, as it is not found in the sacred Canon of their infallible Church; but Protestants, who adhere to the principles of the Reformation, and whose tenure of Christianity is therefore contingent on the appeal to reason, must inevitably enroll Enoch among the prophets, or reconsider the supernatural in Christianity.

It is important for readers of the Book of Enoch to recollect that we owe the Reformation to independent study of sacred literature, previously withdrawn from the people through the oblivion of dead and untranslated languages. The long neglected Book of Enoch now stands in analogous relationship with modern seekers after religious truth; and it remains for its readers to exercise that right of private judgment, to which Protestantism owes its existence, by impartially considering the inevitable modifications of faith involved in the discovery, that the language and ideas of alleged revelation are found in a pre-existent work, accepted by Evangelists and Apostles as inspired, but classed by modern theologians among apocryphal productions.

In revising the proof-sheets of the Book of Enoch, we have been still further impressed by its relationship with New Testament Scripture. Thus, the parable of the sheep, rescued by the good Shepherd from hireling guardians and ferocious wolves, is obviously borrowed by the fourth Evangelist from Enoch 89, in which the author depicts the shepherds as killing and destroying the sheep before the advent of their Lord, and thus discloses the true meaning of that hitherto mysterious passage in John's parable—"All that ever came before me are thieves and robbers"—language in which we now detect an obvious reference to the allegorical shepherds of Enoch.

GOD'S PLAN TO SAVE YOU

The "Son of Man" spoken of in Enoch was revealed in Jesus Christ as both the Messiah and the Son of God (described in the Old Testament, the Book of Enoch, and the New Testament).

The Book of Enoch contains messages of great reward, redemption, and eternal life, but it also carries heavy warnings of eternal destruction and suffering. God knows that humans are imperfect and sinful, so he sent the Son of Man to pay the price for our sin. Jesus took on the suffering you and I deserved, making a way for you to be with God for eternity in paradise. It's time to leave your sin behind.

You can accept Jesus right now by praying this prayer out loud:

> Jesus, I am a sinner. Please forgive me. I believe that you are the son of God, that you died for my sins, and that you rose from the dead. I give my life to you. Be my Lord and my savior.

What now?

First, you must repent of your sins. "Repent" is a fancy way of saying that you turn away from your sins. All Christians make mistakes, but we can also make the conscious decision to turn away from a sinful life and commit ourselves to living the way God wants us to.

Next, find a church that preaches the Bible and believes that the entire Bible is God's true word. Tell someone there that you've given your life to Christ and that you want to be baptized. 1 Peter 3:20-22 tells us that Baptism is tied to the flood of Noah, when God washed away the evils detailed in the Book of Enoch:

"Baptism, which corresponds to this *(Noah's flood)*, now saves you, not as a removal of dirt from the body but as an appeal to God for a good conscience, through the resurrection of Jesus Christ, who has gone into heaven and is at the right hand of God, with angels, authorities, and powers having been subjected to him."

Now find yourself a Bible and read it. Owning a physical copy is recommended, but there are also free Bible phone apps, such as YouVersion, and free computer programs, such as eSword. Many websites also have online and downloadable pdf versions of the Bible. Even if you've read the Bible a hundred times before, you will gain incredible new insight now that you've given your life to Christ.

Here are a few verses to get you started:

1. All Are Lost
for all have sinned and fall short of the glory of God
(Romans 3:23)

2. All Need to Repent
Therefore, repent and turn to him to have your sins blotted out
(Acts 3:19 ISV)

3. All Must Accept Christ
Jesus said to him, "I am the way, and the truth, and the life. No one comes to the Father except through me." (John 14:6)
Truly, I tell all of you with certainty, the one who believes in me has eternal life. (John 6:47 ISV)
For God so loved the world, that he gave his only Son, that whoever believes in him should not perish but have eternal life. (John 3:16)
Because, if you confess with your mouth that Jesus is Lord and believe in your heart that God raised him from the dead, you will be saved. For with the heart one believes and is justified, and with the mouth one confesses and is saved. (Romans 10:9-10)

4. All Should Confess Him as Savior

So everyone who acknowledges me *(Jesus)* before men, I also will acknowledge before my Father who is in heaven, but whoever denies me before men, I also will deny before my Father who is in heaven. (Matthew 10:32-33)

Further Verses:

Just as sin entered the world through one man, and death resulted from sin, therefore everyone dies, because everyone has sinned. (Romans 5:12 ISV)

For the wages of sin is death, but the free gift of God is eternal life in Christ Jesus our Lord. (Romans 6:23)

But if you don't repent, then you, too, will all die. (Luke 13:3 ISV)

Whoever believes in the Son has eternal life; whoever does not obey the Son shall not see life, but the wrath of God remains on him. (John 3:36)

Do you not know that all of us who have been baptized into Christ Jesus were baptized into his death? We were buried therefore with him by baptism into death, in order that, just as Christ was raised from the dead by the glory of the Father, we too might walk in newness of life. For if we have been united with him in a death like his, we shall certainly be united with him in a resurrection like his. (Romans 6:3-5)

Whoever believes in him is not condemned, but whoever does not believe is condemned already, because he has not believed in the name of the only Son of God. (John 3:18)

And Finally:

Believe in the Lord Jesus, and you will be saved, you and your household. (Acts 16:31)

For the grace of God has appeared, bringing salvation to all people. (Titus 2:11)

Now that we have been justified by his blood, how much more will we be saved from wrath through him! For if, while we were enemies, we were reconciled to God through the death of his Son, how much more, having been reconciled, will we be saved by his life! (Rom 5:9-10)

Everyone who calls on the name of the Lord will be saved. (Romans 10:13)

ACCEPT CHRIST TODAY!

www.enochmsv.com

Thank you for using the Book of Enoch MSV,
Modern Standard Version.

Please consider leaving a review of this book on the site where
you purchased it. Customer reviews are the best way to get this
timeless work into the hands of others.

www.ingramcontent.com/pod-product-compliance
Lightning Source LLC
Chambersburg PA
CBHW052126270326
41930CB00012B/2777